The Queen of Portland's Roses

The Life of Georgiana Burton Pittock

by
Janet L. Wilson

Panoply Press
Lake Oswego, Oregon

All rights reserved. No part of this publication may be reproduced or transmitted in any form or by any means, electronically or mechanically, including photocopying, recording, or by any information storage or retrieval system, without prior written permission from the publisher. Permission is not required for brief quotations used in reviews or articles about this book.

Copyright © 2006, 2014 by Janet L. Wilson

Printed in the United States of America.
All rights reserved.

Cover Illustrations: Pittock Mansion- Byron Kibbey
                     Rose Background- Janora Bayot
                     Rose Bouquet- Janora Bayot

Cover & Book Design: Heather Kibbey

ISBN: 978-1-882877-44-7

Panoply Press
PO Box 1885
Lake Oswego, Oregon 97035
panoplypress@gmail.com

*To my friend,
Henry Lewis Pittock II.*

Table of Contents

Preface 6

Introduction 9

Chapter One: The Early Years 11

Chapter Two: Raising a Family 23

Chapter Three: Charities & Good Works 39

Chapter Four: Georgiana's Roses 51

Chapter Five: Georgie's Ships 59

Chapter Six: At Leisure 67

Chapter Seven: Pittock Mansion 75

Chapter Eight: Georgiana's Grandchildren 85

Chapter Nine: Georgiana's Legacy 97

A Pittock Family Album 105

Georgiana Burton's Family Tree 118

Henry Pittock's Family Tree 119

Henry & Georgiana's Family Tree 120

    Daughter Susan Pittock's Family Tree 121

    Son Fred Francis Pittock's Family Tree 122

    Daughter Caroline's ("Carrie") Family Tree 123

    Daughter Katherine's ("Kate") Family Tree 124

    Daughter Helen Louise's ("Lucy") Family Tree 125

Sources 127

Index 129

Acknowledgments 131

About the Author 133

Preface

During the course of my gathering the Pittock family genealogy, Henry Pittock II (Georgiana's grandson) and I became close friends. He was one of the kindest men I have ever known. Henry was a loving son, husband, father and grandfather. He would go completely out of his way to help a friend—and he had many friends.

I could never thank him enough for all the family history, videos and pictures that he has shared with me. If it were not for Henry Lewis Pittock II this book could not have been published. He made me feel like I was part of his family.

When he knew I was coming to visit he would put on the tea pot and I would bring the homemade cookies. Henry especially loved chocolate!

Henry Pittock died in 2006 and is buried at River View Cemetery along with his grandparents, parents, wife, family members and many of the elite of Portland.

I feel privileged to have known Henry and I find peace knowing that he rests with his wife and family. I especially want to thank Henry's children for sharing their father with me and allowing me to spend some time with him to say goodbye the night before he passed.

Janet L. Wilson
Portland, Oregon

Introduction

Georgiana Pittock left an exceptional legacy to the people of Portland, Oregon. For a woman who lived within the confines of Victorian marriage and motherhood, her accomplishments were remarkable. A century later, we still marvel at the wide range of good works she carried out. We appreciate the charitable organizations she founded that have lived long after her death.

But what is perhaps her most significant contribution began at home—right in her own garden. To Oregonians, Georgiana Pittock was truly the Queen of Portland's Roses. She gave to her adopted city a civic identity, a beloved annual celebration and even a splendid nickname!

Georgiana Martin Burton Pittock, one of Portland's early pioneers, was a woman of spirit, seemingly unafraid of any challenge and far ahead of her time. This is her story.

Chapter One:
The Early Years

The year was 1854, a bad year for cholera. The Oregon Trail, stretching almost two thousand miles, from Missouri to the Oregon Territory, was marked with graves on its entire length. But that was the year Elwood Morgan Burton made the decision to come west with his wife, Rhoda Ann Hall Burton and their three young daughters.

The elder Burtons, Elwood (1817-1887) and Rhoda Ann (1820-1896), were both born and raised in the state of New York. Married in 1841 in Watertown, New York, they soon moved to Missouri where they settled down to raise a family.

Their first child, a daughter Helen, was born in 1842. The next daughter, Georgiana Martin Burton was born in Clark County, Missouri, on the fourteenth of November, 1845.

Georgiana was named after her paternal grandfather the Reverend George Burton and her maternal grandmother Alzina Martin Hall. Soon after Georgiana's birth, the family moved to Keokuk, Iowa.

Yet her father, Elwood Burton was restless. In 1849, he followed the lure of the California gold mines, leaving his family behind. He stayed there for two years and during that time came to believe that the west had limitless possibilities. He wanted to make a good life for his growing family and he felt that the west was the best place to do so.

In the mid-nineteenth century, such a rigorous trip often required years of planning, so the Burtons did not leave Missouri to cross the plains until 1854.

The Mystery of Georgiana's Birth Date

The exact date of Georgiana's birth remains a mystery. In fact, we may never know for sure when she was born because birth records in Clark County were lost in a fire. According to family genealogy, Georgiana was born November 14, 1844. However, her tombstone suggests 1843 and her obituary, 1845.

I have chosen to use the obituary date as it coincides best with the birth dates of her children, the 1860 Census and other reference books. Combining this information gives me three sources with the same information, thus making it the most reliable.

This meant that Georgiana was 15 at the time of her marriage (her husband Henry, 26)—not an unusual age then but surprisingly young by later standards. Do the different dates suggest a later cover-up to bring this prominent woman's biography into socially acceptable "compliance"?

Chapter One: The Early Years

By that time, the family had grown to include daughter Jane, born in 1848. Two sons, George and Charles, both died in infancy. When they left in the spring of 1854 with their three young daughters, ages six through eleven, Mrs. Burton was pregnant with their fourth daughter, Mary, who was born in Oregon.

The Burton family, with all their possessions stowed in a wagon that was tiny by today's travel standards, joined a wagon train headed for Oregon. They had no idea before they left that it was a bad year for cholera but once on the trail, the discovery of graves of other pioneers kept fear close at hand.

Many years later, another generation of youngsters in the family enjoyed hearing their grandmother Georgiana fondly recall the story of her trip across the Oregon Trail. There were dangers everywhere, not only the cholera outbreak, but also the unpredictability of communication with Native American tribes. Indeed, crossing the plains must have been a very exciting time for a young girl of nine, especially a child with her own horse.

Helen, Georgiana's older sister, was asked to watch out for little Georgie while they rode alongside the wagon. However, one day while on the trail, Georgie got ahead of the wagon train and was picked up by the local Indians. We can only imagine her parents' grief and what must have gone through Georgiana's mind as well.

The family had no news of her for three days, before the local tribe brought her back, with an offer to purchase the cute and spunky little girl! The natives offered special gifts to Mr. Burton including ponies and moccasins. However he was able to talk them out of the trade, reclaim his daughter and head westward again with his family.

After safely arriving in Portland the family settled down in Milwaukie, Oregon where Mr. Burton started the only flour mill in the area. He operated the mill for about one year and then moved into Portland where he built his family a home on the southwest corner of Second and Salmon Streets in what is now the downtown area.

In 1857, the family moved into their new home. By then, Portland had grown to a little more than a "rest stop"—when the Burtons arrived, there were very few homes and only three dirt roads paralleling the Willamette River.

There were more saloons than churches and the stumps in the streets were painted white so that the drunks could see them at night. This gave the fledgling city its first nickname, *Stumptown*.

But the timing was right for change and Elwood Burton was a man of vision. He could see that Portland would soon have a need for grand new buildings.

Chapter One: The Early Years

The earliest known photograph of Georgiana Burton, at the age of 12 or 13, in her school uniform, Portland, Oregon, c. 1855-56.

Georgiana Martin Burton's middle name came from her maternal grandmother, Alzina Martin Hall.

Chapter One: The Early Years

According to the 1860 census, he considered himself a carpenter, but he joined an architectural firm and eventually became an architect, working on the design of many of Portland's finest structures including the Old Courthouse, Dekum Building, Cook Block, the Old Church, and the First Presbyterian Church. He also was the architect of the Failing, Ladd and Atkinson schools as well as many private homes.

He diversified his enterprises, owning the Stark Street Ferry, a book store that was later known as, J.K. Gill's and a sheep ranch in eastern Oregon. Elwood Burton was a man well respected in the community and successful in his business ventures. His growing family (five children lived to adulthood) wanted for nothing. This is the Portland Georgiana knew and grew up in, watching her Father build and the city grow.

For Georgiana, life was good as she attended the Portland Academy on sixth and Broadway and then the Female Seminary, also in Portland. She was very popular and had a wide circle of friends, ones she would keep all her adult life. The names of her friends come straight from the history of Portland, and today can be found on a map of its streets or a listing of its businesses. They included Mrs. Aaron Meier of Meier & Frank; Sarah Abrams Hogue, from a well-known Portland family; Lizzy Couch (Captain Couch's daughter who married Dr. Rodney Glisan, Glisan Street); Mrs. C.A. Dolph, from a well-known and wealthy family; and Mrs. P.J. Mann (the Mann Mansion).

The Queen of Portland's Roses

It was about this time that Georgiana met Henry Pittock, who was working as a typesetter for the weekly *Oregonian* Newspaper. He was a handsome young man with a clear future who had crossed the plains just two years before.

Georgiana's Surrey with the Fringe on Top

While visiting with William Burton Barry (a Pittock great-nephew) over lunch several years ago, I asked him if his mother ever told him any stories that she had heard from her Aunt Georgie. He told me that Mrs. Pittock loved to tell stories to her nieces while they went for drives. He remembered his mother telling him that Aunt Georgie loved to ride horses and that's how she got in trouble on the plains as her family headed west. She had her own pony and loved fast riding. This is how she got ahead of the wagon train and was captured by Native Americans.

Georgiana was allowed to ride her pony for a few years more until her father said she was now too old to ride astride. Young ladies did not straddle a horse, they rode in a carriage. Mr. Burton then bought his daughter her own surrey that was pulled by one horse. It was a marvelous surrey with fringe on top. She drove it at such high speeds that the fringe would just fly. She was always running errands for her mother and father in her surrey.

Portland at this time had only three streets, so Georgiana often had to go right by *The Oregonian* newspaper office. This is how she met her Henry. After meeting little Georgie, Henry sent a letter to his mother saying, "Mother I have met the sweetest little girl." Shortly thereafter they were wed at Georgie's family home

Chapter One: The Early Years

Georgiana was known as, "mature for her years, handsome, vivacious, frank and outspoken" and it did not take them long to decide to wed. They married in June of 1860 in the home of her parents near Sixth and Jefferson Streets.

Within a few months Georgiana was expecting a child. Henry by then owned the newspaper, having received the business in lieu of back wages when the previous owner wanted out. Henry proved to be a hard worker and an astute businessman, as he struggled to build the *The Oregonian* into a financially viable and successful daily newspaper.

Research tells us that, in December 1860, after six months of marriage, Henry left his bride to travel to San Francisco to purchase a new printing press. He boarded the Constitution, a ship that according to newspaper articles was in poor condition and leaked water badly. Henry slept on a top bunk to stay dry but water wasn't his only concern. There were many storms that month making the water rough and Henry seasick most of the way. The storms also caused the trip to take more than a month instead of its scheduled seven days.

People in Portland had almost given up hope that Henry would return, as they thought the ship had gone down in the rough seas and that all aboard had died. The sixteen-year-old Georgiana must have been very happy and relieved to see her husband, the father of her unborn child, finally come through the door at last.

Life was not always easy in the early years of her marriage. Three times Henry asked his wife for permission to pawn her horse and buggy in order to cover the payroll at *The Oregonian*. Yet with each request, Georgiana did what she had to do to help support her husband in all of his endeavors, through fire, flood, economic downturns and riots.

As their family continued to grow, Henry and Georgiana's wealth and standing in the community grew as well. They were an up-and-coming couple in an up-and-coming town.

Chapter One: The Early Years

The wedding of Georgiana Burton and Henry Pittock,
June 30, 1860. Best man and maid of honor were
George T. Myers and Sarah Abrams.

Young wife and mother, Georgiana B Pittock,
circa 1870.

Chapter Two:
Raising A Family

In 1861, Henry and Georgiana's first child, Susan, was born and others continued to arrive until 1878. Nine children were born to the couple with only six living to maturity (age 21), which was not uncommon for the time.

A Son to Carry on His Name

Henry's namesake died in infancy at ten months of age. After his son's death, Henry became increasingly distressed that he did not have a son to carry on his name. He urged his son, Frederick, to have a son and carry on the family name and, after two marriages and five daughters, Fred finally produced Henry Lewis Pittock II in 1915.

All of the children were born at home, grew up and went to school in Portland. They watched Portland grow and prosper just as their parents did. All but two of the children were baptized at the Unitarian Church at the same time, on September 25th, 1873. The two exceptions were Helen Louise who had not yet been born, and Greta, who had a physical disability.

The Pittock children, and later the grandchildren, were the highlight of the family and the family lived a comfortable life, with all they needed or wanted. They were deeply involved with the Unitarian Church and would perform at the church. Kate sang in the choir and Lucy played the piano. Even little Roby recited poems at the church. The Burton home was close by and the children often visited grandmother and grandfather Burton.

The Pittocks were generous and warm-hearted. Two of Georgiana's widowed sisters died at an early age. Carrie Burton Gallien had three children (Elwood and twins Louise and and Charles). Louise came to live with her Aunt Georgie. Maria Van Houten had only one child, Helen, who also came to live with the Pittocks.

The nieces were well cared for. One story tells us about Louise, who was all dressed up for a holiday dinner and while she was at the table, the cook's helper accidentally spilled something on her pretty dress. Louise was upset but Mrs. Pittock told her she would buy her a whole new outfit to make up for the accident.

The nieces remember, too, that Henry always had tickets for all the children whenever the circus or any other event came to town.

It was not a life without grief. In addition to the infants who had died, the Pittocks lost their adored son, Roby, who became ill while back east at college and died at the age of twenty.

Chapter Two: Raising A Family

A group photograph at the Burton home in Portland c. 1890. Georgiana's mother, Rhoda Ann, is seated at left; grandmother, Alzina Hall is at center with servants.
Two of Georgiana's sisters are at right and second from left.

However it was a life filled with great joy as well, as one can see in pictures of the family on hikes, picnics or vacations. No matter how busy Georgiana was with her household duties or her charitable work, there was always time for fun. In later years, Mr. and Mrs. Pittock loved having their pictures taken with the grandchildren. There are several photos of the proud grandparents cuddling an infant—or two. You can see the light of love in their eyes when they are looking at the grandchildren.

For most of their lives, Georgiana and Henry lived in modest homes. In 1856, Henry had bought a large parcel of land for $300, in what is now downtown Portland, but which was then a wooded retreat. Over the years, the Pittocks built several homes on the land. The first was a quiet cottage at 6th and Morrison, the second at 3rd and Morrison, and then 4th and Salmon. Then in 1864, they built the home they would live in for half a century, an unpretentious home bounded by Washington and Stark, West Park and 10th.

Their grown children lived in homes that the Pittocks had vacated. By the time they built their last home, up the hill in Imperial Heights (the home we now call Pittock Mansion), the city of Portland had surrounded their country acreage. Instead of a quiet little cottage accessible by a path through the woods, the land, now dotted with Pittock homes, was surrounded by a modern industrialized city. Today, part of that acreage is known as the "Pittock Block" and there is no sign of the colony of homes that had once been there.

Chapter Two: Raising A Family

Two views of the Pittock home in the land that later became known as the "Pittock Block." The other homes were occupied by family members. Henry and Georgiana named their house, "Maple Grove," after surrounding the block with maple trees.

GEORGIANA AND HENRY'S FAMILY

Susan Agnes Pittock (1861-1952)

Georgiana's oldest child, Susan, was known as a very modern woman for her time. She loved to travel and to read—in fact all of Henry and Georgiana's children and grandchildren were avid readers. Susan followed in many of her Mother's footsteps in the field of charity work. She married Frank C. Middleton (1845-1916) in Portland on November 16, 1881. They had two children: Francis (1888-1892) born in Portland and Harry (Hal) born in California. In 1909, after divorcing her first husband, Susan married E. Fred Emery (1862-1948). They had no children.

Four generations gathered on the steps of the Burton home for this photograph: *(at left)* Susan Pittock Middleton with her son, Francis; Georgiana Pittock *(center)* and her mother, Rhoda Ann Burton.

Chapter Two: Raising A Family

In 1941, all of the family gathered in California to celebrate Susan's 80th birthday. We have video in the archives showing her looking good and getting around very well. Susan lived to be 90. Fred and Susan had a lovely home on the Willamette River.

Greta Pittock (1863- ?)

A mystery surrounds the second of the Pittock children, daughter Greta. She does not show up on any genealogy charts. There are no birth or death records to be found. Over the years, there have been many questions about the mere existence of Greta and theories about her "disappearance." However, in Georgiana's obituary, her lifelong friend states that the Pittocks did have nine children. Pictures including Greta as part of a family group have been found (among Pittock family photo albums) up to around the year, 1918. She would have been around 55 years old and still alive when Mrs. Pittock passed.

After more than two decades of research, the author believes that Greta suffered from epilepsy and was hidden from the public since this was at the time considered to be a shameful condition. There was then no effective treatment for this disorder and very little understanding of the causes. Today Greta might have taken a pill and lived a perfectly normal life, but a hundred years ago, she and her family went to great effort to avoid the stigma of society. Although this family secret has been well hidden and no further evidence of Greta has been found, her name was carried on by her niece, Dorothy Leadbetter Teren, when she named her daughter Greta in 1936.

Frederick Francis Pittock (1864-1938)

Fred was Henry and Georgiana's first son and the only son to reach maturity. Fred was the official "bookkeeper" for his father's estate, frozen for 20 years after Henry died. He was responsible for disbursing cash allowances monthly to the family members from Henry's will. However Fred died two years before the will was finally released.

Fred first married Catherine West and adopted a child they named Alice. They divorced and then in 1903 Fred married Bertha Comings Leadbetter (1873-1971). This union produced six children:

Virginia Comfort Pittock Thorsen (1905-1985);
Marjorie Ann Pittock McDougall (1907-1999);
Barbara Faire Pittock Johnsrud (1908-1991);
Roberta Ruth Pittock MacNaughton (1909-1989);
Fredrika Faith Pittock (1912-1996) Woodbridge/
       Behrendt / O'Leary / Williams;
and finally Henry (Hank) Lewis Pittock II (1915-2007).

As a token of their love and gratitude, Henry and Georgiana gave Fred and Bertha one million dollars...so came young Henry's nickname of "The Million-Dollar Baby."

Georgiana's grandson Henry's first job was at the Oregonian newspaper. In June, 1939, he married Peggy Janet Victors. Henry loved sports and competed in almost every field imaginable. He loved cars, travel and researching family genealogy. He retired from banking and moved to Cannon

Beach in 1972. Henry and Peggy had four children: Henry Pittock III, Diane, Peter and Pam.

Fred Francis, Georgiana & Henry's only surviving son, shown here in his teens.

Robert (Roby) Elwood Pittock (1866-1886)

Roby, as he was affectionately called, was away at school when he became ill and died of typhoid pneumonia at age twenty. His father had been grooming him to take over helm of *The Oregonian*.

The Queen of Portland's Roses

Pittock son, Robert ("Roby") became ill and died at age 20, while away at school.

Roby's death came as a great shock for the couple, as they had lost children in infancy but never in young adulthood. Henry and Georgiana immediately caught a train heading east to meet the train with Roby's body onboard. It took over a week to get the body back to Portland. The funeral service was held in their home. Roby had never married.

Caroline (Carrie) Thuseba Pittock Leadbetter (1870-1972)

Carrie and Frederick Leadbetter, married in 1893, were the parents of five children:

Georgiana C. Leadbetter / Andreae / D'Albuquerque (1885-1975)

Chapter Two: Raising A Family

Frederick William Leadbetter, Jr. (1896-1897)

Henry Lewis Pittock Leadbetter (1900-1989) who married Constance Williams

Dorothy Rose Leadbetter Teren (1902-1992)

Mary Elizabeth ("Betty") Leadbetter Cronin/ Meier (1904-   )

When her father's will called for a 20-year freeze of his assets, Caroline Pittock Leadbetter fought the will by taking it all the way to the Supreme Court. However the will was never broken. Carrie lived a comfortable life with several luxurious estates and at least two expensive yachts. She had different sets of servants for each of her different homes. She lived to be 102 years old, and her daughter, Betty, has exceeded that. Betty, who is still living at the time of this publication*, is now 110 and gave up driving at about age 100!

Henry Lewis Pittock Jr. (1871-1871)

Henry's namesake died in infancy at ten months of age.

Katherine Thorne Pittock (1873-1941) Hertzman/Hebard

Kate's first husband died in 1907 after seven years of marriage. They had one son, John Jr., (1902-1903). Kate then married Lockwood Hebard at the mansion in, 1914. The Hebards had no children and lived at Pittock Mansion.

Kate was the president of The Oregonian Publishing Company when she passed away. She also served, prior to that, as her father's private secretary while he was living.

* Sadly, Betty Meier passed away in 2014, just after the printing of this edition.

The Queen of Portland's Roses

Kate was passionate about her music and would sing to entertain guests at her parent's home and at the Unitarian Church where she was a member of the choir. It was at the church that she met her second husband, Lockwood.

Four of the Pittock daughters, c. 1900, *(from left)*: Caroline, Helen Louise ("Lucy"), Susan and Kate

She continued to support many of the charities that her mother had been involved in. Kate loved to knit and put together puzzles. In 1894 she climbed Mt. Hood with her sister Lucy and her father, who was then at the age of 60. All three were members of the Mazamas, a Northwest mountaineering organizaton of which Henry was a founding member.

Helen Louise ("Lucy") Pittock (1875-1945) Gantenbein

Lucy and her husband, J. Edward Ganteinbein lived at the mansion with their three children: Rhoda Jane Gantenbein

Chapter Two: Raising A Family

Adams (1909-1977); Georgiana Gantenbein Aston (1912-1985); and Robert (Peter) Pittock Gantenbein (1914-1984).

Lucy loved to travel and climb mountains with her father and sister. She also carried on the tradition that her mother had started in the field of charity work. Lucy loved to play the piano and, in fact, played the one that is displayed today at Pittock Mansion. She also loved to knit, put together puzzles and work on cross word puzzles. Half-done puzzles and an open dictionary often lay about the house.

Lucy and her family lived in the mansion with her sister, Kate and Lockwood Hebard. Lucy's son Peter was the last descendant to live in the mansion.

Harriet Lovell Pittock (1878-1878)
Harriet died in infancy at 4 months of age. She was named after one of Henry's sisters and was the last child to be born to Henry and Georgiana.

THE NIECES

Two of Mrs. Pittock's nieces lived at Pittock Mansion, and today there is a room in the Mansion known as "The Nieces' Room."

Mrs. Pittock had two younger sisters, Maria L. Burton and Carrie T. Burton, who, sadly, died before their time, leaving behind four children in need of a home.

The Queen of Portland's Roses

Maria Lola (not to be confused with her sister Maria Elizabeth who died in infancy) married Garret Van Houten, from New Jersey, who had come to Portland in 1887 and who was well known as a representative of a real estate business. Maria and Garret were married in August of 1892. They had only one child, a daughter, Helen.

They were married for a only few years before Mr. Van Houten died, leaving Maria a widow. Maria passed away in1879 and family has said she was in a wheel chair most of her life. Helen lived with her Aunt Carrie and her three children before going to live with Aunt Georgie.

Georgiana's other sister, Carrie T. Burton, married Mr. Charles L. Gallien. Charles was born in New Zealand on a large sheep ranch and came to America in the 1880s. Charles and Carrie met in Portland, where they both attended the Presbyterian Church, and they married in April of 1889. Three children came of this marriage Elwood H. Gallien (who married Selene Kropp) and the twins, Louise and Charles.

Carrie also became a widow in 1907, after Charles died in Italy while there on business. He had been a bookkeeper by trade. Carrie passed away in 1913, just before the mansion was finished. After her death, Louise came to live with Aunt Georgie.

Charles, however, felt he was old enough to live on his own, and he left town to join the circus. He later married a woman by the name of Beatrice Wilcox.

Chapter Two: Raising A Family

Georgiana's nieces, *(l. to r.)* Helen Van Houton and Louise Gallien, came to live with the Pittocks after the death of their widowed mothers, Georgiana's sisters, Maria Lola and Carrie.

Louise married Alexander Barry and had two children, Alexander and William Burton Barry, who was born on January 19th, 1927. He served in the Navy during World War II and passed away in 2002. I had the pleasure of interviewing Mr. Barry on three separate occasions. He had such fond memories of the mansion and enjoyed sharing family secrets. He still remembered riding up and down in the dumbwaiter, although his brother made him go first to see if it would hold their weight.

The Queen of Portland's Roses

A family gathering at Fern Lodge, Camas, c. 1916. This is one of the few photographs of Georgiana and Henry's daughter, Greta, who stands at left, behind her father (holding Henry II). Next to Greta is Fred's wife, Bertha, then *(l. to r.)* Fred Pittock, a female nurse, Susan Pittock Emery and Caroline Pittock Leadbetter. Georgiana sits center front.

Chapter Three:
Charities & Good Works

As children do, Mrs. Pittock's children were growing up fast and becoming more independent all the time. This allowed Georgiana even more freedom to indulge in her favorite charities, most of which were centered under the umbrella of the Unitarian Church. Having a Chinese cook named Himmi, did not hurt either. Charity work had become the "fashionable" thing to do when you had reached the financial comfort level and community status that Mrs. Pittock realized at this time in her life.

Fashionable a philosophy or not, it was a guiding principle of Mrs. Pittock's life. She believed in making a difference in the lives of the innocent children, with the hope for a better society in general. Keeping families together was a priority for Georgiana and she often would take money from her own bank account to buy a train ticket to help a child get back home to any family she might have left even, if it was on the east coast.

How fascinating it is that so many of the charitable organizatiions Georgiana Pittock helped to found, or was a member of, one hundred years ago, still serve the citizens of Portland today.

LADIES SEWING SOCIETY

It was in August of 1873 when Mrs. Pittock joined the Unitarian Church in downtown Portland. That very same year all her children were baptized at the Unitarian Church were baptized at the Unitarian Church on the same day, December 25th 1873.

The Ladies' Sewing Society also known as The Ladies' Relief Society made money by sewing baby clothes and selling them at bazaars. This was a very good way for the ladies to raise enough money to help out needy families in the area.

Mrs. Pittock was known for organizing spectacular bazaars. Her first bazaar was held in 1887 and was advertised in *The Oregonian* Newspaper as the Christmas Bazaar not to be missed. She held another bazaar in 1902 that was credited with making enough money to keep the church from closing because of financial difficulties.

During her life time Mrs. Pittock was a very active member of the church. She sat on several advisory committees, served as vice-president, and then president of the Ladies' Sewing Society.

The society carries on today as the First Church's Alliance and is located at 1011 SW 12th, Portland, Oregon. This institution is still an asset to our community and a leader in helping the people of this city.

Chapter Three: Charities & Good Works

The Unitarian Church's Ladies Sewing Society, shown here in this 1887 photograph, was known for its charitable works, benefitting Portland's less fortunate. Georgiana Pittock is seated in the second row from the front, second from right.

41

The Queen of Portland's Roses

FRUIT AND FLOWER DAY CARE

As more and more single women with children started entering the workplace, it became clear that a day care for children was a necessity in Portland. Starting in 1885, from deliveries of baskets of fruit and flowers to "shut-ins" in hospitals and gifts of food and clothing to the poor farm, the Fruit and Flower Day Care became a reality in 1906.

This was the first day care center in Oregon. Open from 7 am to 7 pm they charged 10 cents a day for single women and 25 cents a day if both parents worked. The children were seen by a doctor and vaccinated before entry. They were also given a dose of cod liver oil just before nap time. Children came in the morning not wanting to stay and in the evening they did not want to go.

Mrs. Pittock believed whole heartedly that this was very important service to the working public and especially to young women who had to earn a living. Georgiana was a life long member giving of her time and talents plus $100.00 per year out of her own funds, to help support the center. Her children and grandchildren continued to support this worthy cause. The center is still a delightful and inviting atmosphere for children to learn and grow.

The Fruit and Flower Day Care Center is still in operation and is located at 2378 NW Irving Portland, Oregon.

Chapter Three: Charities & Good Works

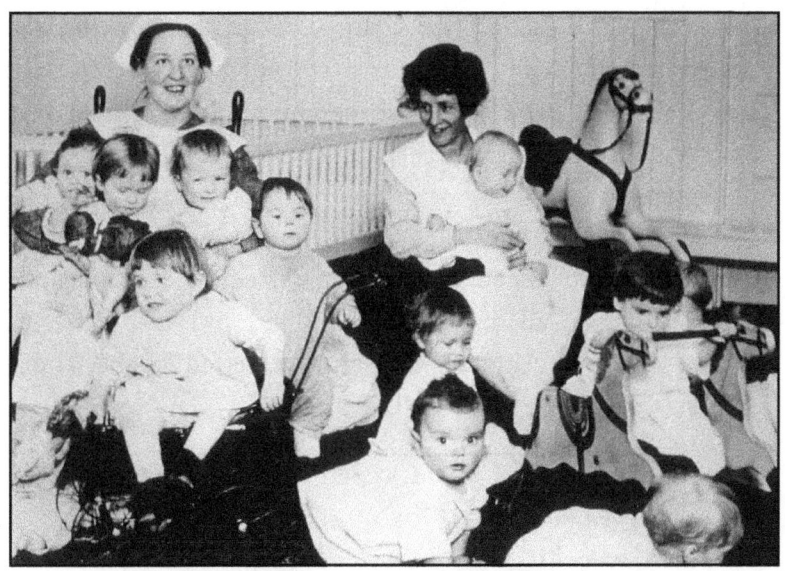

Fruit and Flower Day Care was one of Georgiana's favorite charitable causes. It still provides care for children today in Portland.

THE BABY HOME

Mrs. Pittock's favorite charity was the Baby Home organized in, 1888. This home for babies was where Georgiana spent most of her energy. Many babies were being left on the front steps of churches and homes. They were the children of unwed mothers or children of fathers whose wives had died. Others had lost their parents on the wagon trains coming west and had no family here to care for them.

This was very distressing to Georgiana. She used the efforts of the Ladies Sewing Society to make large amounts of clothes for the babies. She also held bazaars, even in her home, to raise money for the orphaned babies by selling some of the clothes they had made. She charged 10 cents admission and sold a variety of items including a 10 cent baby clothes. She even challenged her friends and neighbors to bake their best desserts and bring them to be auctioned to the highest bidder.

One of her largest and most famous bazaars was held at the Marquam Theater. She had fresh flower decorations, refreshments of all kinds, fairy lights and an orchestra. Admission was 50 cents this time and she netted $54.60, a huge success!

The Baby Home, Georgiana's favorite charitable cause.

The name of the Baby Home was changed to The Waverly Baby Home in 1944, for the name of the neighborhood where it is located, 3550 SE Woodward Street Portland, Oregon. Mrs. Pittock's daughters Susan and Lucy were life long members.

Chapter Three: Charities & Good Works

MARTHA WASHINGTON HOTEL

The Martha Washington Hotel was a hotel for single working women. Advertisements in the paper read "Young women arriving in the city without friends to meet her or women in Portland without family ties are eagerly invited." To be accepted you and to present a satisfactory testimonial of character and agree to a two-page list of rules. Among the rules was the fact that gentlemen were received only on Sundays and Wednesday. You could not exceed more than ten pieces of laundry per week and the front doors were locked promptly at 10pm!

In 1894, the hotel was in financial trouble and the executive committee decided to have an elegant fair like none had seen before. It was so large they rented the Exposition building. There were various booths and stages spread throughout the building.

As reported in the newspaper, "Mrs. Pittock and Mrs. Hegele were in charge of the Egyptian Dance", a very risqué number for the time. This venture was a huge success and grossed $7000 for the hotel.

In 1911 the hotel had outgrown its capacity and a new, much larger hotel was commissioned. The new location was at 1802 SW 10th. After the expansion of Portland State University the hotel was moved to 11th and Main. Eventually, the need for such sheltered living conditions diminished and the building was sold.

BOYS' AND GIRLS' AID SOCIETY

Georgiana was a member of the Boys' and Girls' Aid Society and worked alongside her neighbor and friend, the Reverend Thomas Lamb Eliot. While enlisting the help of the Ladies' Aid Society she was an advisory board member with the duties of raising funds for the children.

Georgiana was an advisory board Member of the Boys' and Girls' Aid Society.

The home took in orphaned and or abused children aged three days to sixteen years. The older children took care of the younger ones and all learned to help out around the home. The older girls learned to do laundry and the boys learned to split wood. They all helped out in their garden, which supplied fresh vegetables and fruit. Upon being admitted to the home all were seen by a physician and were given clean and proper clothing.

It wasn't all work though; the children often went on picnics, outings to Multnomah Falls and boat excursions on the river. Even, Christmas trees and presents were donated to the children by the caring citizens of Portland.

Chapter Three: Charities & Good Works

Homes were found as quickly as possible for the children and ads ran in *The Oregonian* describing the children to perspective parents. The new parents were scrutinized thoroughly before placement of any child and final adoption was postponed for six months to see how the child fared in his new home.

This worthy cause is still helping children find loving homes and it located on Boundary Court in Portland, Oregon.

THE PARRY CENTER FOR CHILDREN

Death was so prevalent on the wagon trains west you could find the trail by the graves along the way. The hard trip caused many children to be left orphaned while still on the trail. Some of these children were living with other members of the wagon train until they came into Portland. Once these children were here many were left to fend for themselves on the streets.

The Parry Center, an early Portland orphanage, was also known as The Children's Home.

This need was filled with the help of the Parry Center for Children, also known as The Children's Home, an orphanage founded in 1867 by Elizabeth Parry. Elizabeth working closely with the Ladies Relief Society of which Mrs. Pittock was a member. Children here, as in all of the other homes, were given medical care, clean clothes and a place to live until a suitable home could be found.

The Parry Center is still providing a loving home for challenged children.

PORTLAND WOMEN'S UNION

The Portland Women's Union was established in May of 1887. Their primary goal was to help self-supporting women to help themselves. Mrs. Pittock was not only a board member, she was chair of the finance committee and the fourth president of the Union. In an era where women were not supposed to even lift their skirts enough to keep them dry in the rain, (they were told to stay home when it rained) Mrs. Pittock forged on with women's rights.

In 1850 the first National Women's Rights Convention was held and subsequent conventions were held every year after that. Twelve resolutions were adopted calling for equal treatment of men and women under the law and voting rights for women.

Mrs. Pittock saw Colorado grant the vote to women in 1893, then Utah and Idaho in 1896. Washington State granted

Chapter Three: Charities & Good Works

women the right in 1910 then on to California in 1911. The power of women's rights was growing but the women in Oregon could not vote, until 1912.

OLD PEOPLE'S HOME

There seemed to be almost a home for everyone in Portland, now. There was the Baby Home for babies, the Children's Home for children, The Parry Center for challenged youth and the Boys and Girls Society for adoption. There was a home for working women that did not have families. Then there were homes for old men and old women but there was no home for old, married couples. Some of these couples had been married for so many years that the prospect of living without their spouse caused great despair.

The Old People's Home was established when Mrs. Pittock and Mrs. John Mann recognized the need for elderly couples to remain together.

The Queen of Portland's Roses

Georgiana Pittock spent great amounts of time and effort to help the
needy of Portland. Even her favorite leisure activities—
like puttering in her rose garden—often became the means
to raise funds for a deserving cause.

Chapter Four:
Georgiana's Roses

Who could know, until years later, that the day the Unitarian Church announced its "European Travel" lecture, would be one of the more significant days in Portland history!

Now that Georgiana's children were in school, she discovered that she had more time for her church and her charitable activities. She had time to enjoy her garden, especially the roses, which were, by far, her favorite flowers.

She also had time for for entertainment. When the Unitarian Church announced a lecture on the topic of European Travel, to include the wonderful sights to be seen in England, Georgiana attended eagerly.

To her delight, she learned about fabulous rose gardens and grand rose shows in England. The lure of that country was strong for someone who loved roses as much as Georgiana. She was fascinated by the notion that the British were even holding competition for the best roses, a practice unheard of in Oregon.

Georgiana was inspired by it all and she decided to take a trip with her husband, Henry, who had been born in England,

The Queen of Portland's Roses

to see for herself the glorious roses. While there, she attended a rose show, which gave her many ideas to take home. She knew that the climate in Portland was excellent for growing roses; her own garden thrived in the mild Pacific Northwest and she thought that these kind of events would be good for Oregon too.

In 1888, Georgiana unofficially organized a Rose Society. group that still blooms today. Many of her friends joined the club, each one trying to grow a bigger and/or better rose than her neighbor. Competition was stiff even though it was just for fun. By the very next year, Mrs. Pittock had constructed a tent in her back yard to judge the roses that were being grown, in Portland.

She charged admission and turned the event into a fund raiser for her church. They did not know it at the time but these ladies in long skirts and white gloves had started a tradition that would last for decades to come. This was the beginning of what we know now as Portland's Rose Festival.

Georgiana's first rose competition and exhibition in 1889 was a sizeable event in the growing young city and it drew plenty of attention and interest. Since it was a fundraising success and great entertainment, the event grew larger and more exciting each year.

The floral parade was a natural extension of the rose exhibitions. The year 1906 saw the introduction of the first official, "Rose Festival and Flower Parade."

Chapter Four: Georgiana's Roses

Henry Pittock, in his role as a Royal Rosarian, is shown here with the
Royal Court at Portland's famous Rose Festival,
the event Georgiana Pittock began in her own yard.
Family sources say that two of the little girls shown
in front of Henry were his granddaughters.

The Queen of Portland's Roses

Mrs. Pittock and her neighbors would strip all the roses from their yards to decorate the cars, horses and floats that were in the parade each year, except for the best roses that were saved for competition.

One of the most beautiful entries that year was by Jessee Currey, who was one of the organizers of the Royal Rosarians. Currey also established Portland's now-celebrated International Rose Test Gardens in 1917. Newspaper articles, of the day, credit Mrs. Pittock with inspiring the Rose Festival calling her the "Grande dame of Portland society" in our beautiful Portland, city of roses.

In this c.1915 photograph, *(second from left)* Georgiana and Henry's granddaughter, Barbara Faire Pittock (later Johnsrud) takes part in the Rose Festival celebration.
Barbara was the third daughter of the Pittock's son, Fred Francis.

Chapter Four: Georgiana's Roses

1906 was an exciting year for Portlanders: the Lewis and Clark Exposition was held at that time, and it included, "The greatest amateur rose show ever seen in America," the newspapers reported, with "thousands in attendance."

The Portland Rose Society was officially established in 1902 and is the oldest exclusive rose organization in the United States. Their vision is the same as it was in Mrs. Pittocks' time. Their mission statement, "The glory of the rose would be perpetuated through the years by Portlanders for Portland."

When, in 1914, Georgiana moved from her home in downtown Portland to their newly constructed mansion on Imperial Heights, she moved all her roses with her. They were planted near the Gate Lodge, but none of the old roses still survives to this day. Many were lost when the land slid near the retaining wall of the Gate Lodge and when the new road was put in for the public.

Georgiana Pittock always loved having fresh roses and other flowers in her homes. That was one of the reasons that the greenhouses were built at the mansion. Mrs. Pittock wanted fresh flowers in her home, year round.

Georgiana's favorite rose was called "Moonstone" and Kate had a favorite (named for her) called, "Kate's New Dawn". Susan also had a flower named for her, it was clematis, the Susan P. Emery. Although Georgiana's original roses are gone, Portland Parks Department's horticulturists, along with a team of dedicated Oregon State University Master Gardeners, have created magnificent perennial borders at Pittock Mansion that include rose varieties, such as *Georgiana*, and *The Oregonian*, in honor of Mrs. Pittock. Also planted have been some of the early roses that lined Portland streets in 1906, including Madame Testout and Cecile Brünner.

Georgiana's name and memory are reflected in her final garden, in Portland's Rose Festival tradition, and in The Rose City's timeless love of roses.

Chapter Four: Georgiana's Roses

One of the original greenhouses at Pittock Mansion,
near the site of the present-day parking lot.

In Georgiana's Garden

Georgiana Pittock loved roses. So it's natural for people to ask what varieties of roses she cultivated in her garden. And the answer is, simply, we don't know. There are no known lists of her favorites, or notes complaining of those she found troublesome. After all, black spot is not a new affliction!

However, there are a few clues as to likely candidates. Certainly roses in her early gardens would be older varieties of shrub roses, many brought to Oregon by pioneers. Before leaving for the rigors of a trip across the plains, they'd take cuttings of well-loved roses and poke the short stems into potatoes, where they'd stay moist and could start to root.

With its drifts of small pink blossoms, the popular polyantha Cecile Brünner, introduced in 1881, would surely have found a place in the Pittock rosebeds.

Hybrid teas were introduced in Georgiana's day and it's likely that she would have wanted to own the first hybrid tea of all, LaFrance.

Then there was the climbing hybrid tea that showed up in gardens throughout Portland in that era: the pale pink climber, Madam Caroline Testout (1901).

And according to oral interviews of family members, Georgiana maintained that her favorite rose of all was one she called Moonstone, although this was not the later hybrid of that same name.

Chapter Five:
Georgie's Ships

---

*M*ost of us never get to see our name emblazoned on the stern of a ship. Georgiana Pittock, however, was the namesake for not one, but two steamships! Of course it helped to have a husband whose business interests were extensive. By the beginning of the twentieth century, the Pittocks were well established in the ranks of the Portland elite. Henry had diversified his holdings and Georgiana was a logical recipient of this honor.

THE GEORGIE BURTON

Most people around town knew her as "Mrs. H.L. Pittock." Her close friends called her "Georgiana," but to HenryPittock she was his "little Georgie Burton." And so, in 1906, the ship previously known as the Albany (1896) was named the *Georgie Burton.*

The *Georgie Burton* was launched in San Francisco the day of the infamous earthquake. She was a 154-foot, 382-ton steamer owned by the Western Transportation Company, of which Henry Pittock was a director. But what a day for a launching! The ship was lucky to get out of port before it was damaged by the quake.

The Queen of Portland's Roses

The steamship *Georgie Burton* was launched in San Francisco the day of the great earthquake and was lucky to get out of port without damage. She spent her entire career pushing pulp-and-paper-laden barges on the Columbia and Willamette Rivers, and kept the Oregonian well supplied with newsprint.

Chapter Five: Georgie's Ships

Henry, a practical man and successful business owner, had a reason for his interest in steamships: newsprint for the growing Oregonian newspaper. In fact, the *Georgie Burton* spent her whole career pushing pulp-and-paper-laden barges on the Columbia and Willamette Rivers insuring that Henry had plenty of paper for his daily print run.

After forty-one years of service, the *Georgie Burton* made one last run in, 1947. It was decided that the ship would become a museum at the Marine Park to be built on the riverfront at The Dalles. A gala event was held on board as the ship slowly steamed past waving crowds along the banks of the river all the way to the locks at Bonneville Dam. The decks were full of people who had worked on the ship or had been long-time passengers.

After reaching The Dalles, all the passengers left the ship for the last time, to go to the hotel for dinner, leaving the *Georgie Burton* in a turning basin in The Dalles-Celilo Canal. The ship was to stay in the basin until the high water period in May or June when it would be easier to float the vessel into a cradle and beach it at the site where it would remain forever.

However on Memorial Day in May 1948, before the ship could be moved to its permanent location, there was a huge water surge. A flood that came with such force that the *Georgie Burton* was swept from her mornings and crashed mid-stream on a reef below the canal. The ship's back was broken beyond repair and the *Georgie Burton* could not be refloated again. A sad ending for such a hardworking steamer.

The Queen of Portland's Roses

After 41 years of service, the steamer Georgie Burton was retired and destined to become a museum. However she came to an untimely end on Memorial Day in 1948. A surge of flood water swept her onto a reef below The Dalles-Celilo Canal and she was never able to be refloated

Chapter Five: Georgie's Ships

THE GEORGIANA

Not only were ships named after Georgiana, but she was also delighted to have two granddaughters share her name. So the steamer *Georgiana*, launched in 1914, was actually named after three Georgianas: Mrs. Henry Pittock and her granddaughters Georgiana Gantenbein and Georgiana Leadbetter. What a gala it must have been with all three Georgianas present at the launching of their namesake!

The steamer, Georgiana, was named after not one, but three Georgianas: Mrs. Pittock and two of her granddaughters, Georgiana Gantenbein and Georgiana Leadbetter.

The *Georgiana* had to make good use of space, as she was a trim 145 feet long with a 22 ½ foot beam. Designed for passenger day travel, she had a main lounge, a smoking room with a small galley and a dining room.

The ship was owned by Harkins Transportation Company, another one of Henry Pittock's investments. *Georgiana* was designed for inexpensive ransportation that was clean,

63

safe, speedy and comfortable. Big Pullman-style seats by the windows allowed easy viewing of the fast-moving Columbia River. For just one dollar you could travel from Portland to Astoria. Passengers were encouraged to bring a picnic lunch to enjoy along the five-and-a-half-hour trip. Leaving the dock at 8 am sharp, the ship did not return until 9 or 10 pm, depending on the tide.

Many people took advantage of the inexpensive fare and made it an all-day family outing, for there was plenty to see in Astoria, Seaside, and North Beach. As the mode of transportation changed over the years it was difficult for the *Georgiana* to operate profitably with the passenger trade; even adding a night run and increasing the price of tickets did not boost profits sufficiently. The train and the automobile had now become the way to travel.

Eventually, the *Georgiana* left the lower Columbia River and was renamed the *SS Lake Bonneville* after being remodeled for excursion service by Ralph Staehli, the father of Portland architect, Alfred Staehli, FAIA. The whole Staehli family helped to run the seasonal operation.

One night after the 1940 season, while the ship was berthed in her moorage near the Sellwood Bridge, she took on water and sank. Insurance would have provided funds to float her, but not sufficient money to complete the rehabilitation, so eventually the steamer was traded for moorage charges and was subsequently scrapped.

Chapter Five: Georgie's Ships

All that remains, to our knowledge, are the port and starboard running lanterns, along with posters and freight packets still owned by Mr. Alfred Staehli, who speaks fondly of his days spent on the *SS Bonneville*. He does regret, however, that he did not keep the *Bonneville*'s bell and whistle.

Chapter Six:
At Leisure

From wagon train to airplane, Georgiana must have thought that she'd seen it all in her lifetime. She loved adventure and travel, as did her husband; after all, they had each crossed the Oregon Trail at an early age.

When Georgiana Burton first arrived in Oregon, a horse and buggy was her means of travel, but before her death she had traveled by ship, train and automobile, although she did decline a mule ride while visiting the Grand Canyon. She had even seen an airplane fly over Portland during the Lewis and Clark Exposition of 1905. That must have been a day to remember!

Family outings were a particular favorite of Georgiana's and the family would often gather for a picnic. After the opening of Vista House and the Columbia Scenic Highway, the Pittocks held a picnic at Multnomah Falls. Another, excuse for a picnic would be after a ride to Camas, Washington to see her daughter, Carrie and son, Fred—both families lived at Lacamas Lake, about 25 miles from the mansion.

Mountain climbing was a popular recreation for Henry and his daughters. (Henry was one of the founders of the Mazamas, a mountaineering organization). But climbing peaks was much too strenuous for Georgie. She preferred her church work, lectures, and concerts.

The family could always travel by ship to locations like San Francisco and did so frequently. River cruises to Astoria were popular. But nothing did more to enhance the ease of travel than when the railroad made its way to Portland in 1883. With the arrival of the trains, journeys were so much easier and safer that the Pittock family traveled even more often.

On one trip they took the train to San Diego and met with Henry's brother, Thomas, and sister-in-law Emma at the Hotel Del Coronado. This lovely hotel opened in 1888 and was the talk of the whole Northwest. The Hotel Del Coronado is still open to this day. They went on to see the sights of Mexico after their stay in California. At one point the Pittock family had a second home in Santa Barbara.

Another Pittock trip was one that took them back east to Pittsburgh, where Henry had grown up, after his family had emigrated from England. He wanted to see his family's home and visit relatives. Neville Island in Pennsylvania is where Henry's brother and his family lived and it was a great place to go in the summer.

The World's Fair, which was held in various locations every few years, was a favorite to see. The Pittock family was delighted when it was Portland's turn to host the fair as they would not have to travel far. This was the biggest event to ever take place in Portland, causing the region's population to soar.

Chapter Six: At Leisure

The Pittock family loved to picnic as this group photo, c. 1900, attests. Henry Pittock can be seen at the right of the photo *(middle level)*.

The Queen of Portland's Roses

Georgiana on outings with her sisters: *(top)* at Celilo; *(bottom)* at Cloud Cap, Mt. Hood. *(Georgiana is 2nd from left)*

Chapter Six: At Leisure

Although Georgiana tended to get seasick, she and her family did go to Hawaii on at least one occasion. They explored the Lava Caves, played on the beach and toured the Islands. There was also a trip abroad to see England and a few neighboring countries.

When the automobile arrived in Portland motoring became very popular. Henry and Georgiana never had a barn or horses at Imperial Heights (what we now call Pittock Mansion), only cars, but Henry did keep a horse that was boarded at Witch Hazel Stables & Race Track in Hillsboro, Oregon.

While the automobile is often taken for granted today, in the early days of Pittock Mansion, motoring was a prime source of entertainment. By the time the family moved to Imperial Heights, they no longer kept horses but relied on motorcars. (Henry is in back.)

The Queen of Portland's Roses

On a 1906 adventure in Hawaii, the Pittocks cruised to the island *(top)*, where Henry and Georgiana *(above)* strolled beneath the palms and explored lava caves *(below, at left)*.

Chapter Six: At Leisure

Georgiana was very fond of the automobile and often went on road trips with all the family, with never an empty seat in the car. This was an excellent and inexpensive way to travel with all the new roads that had recently been built. Georgiana liked to sit in the back seat wearing a dust coat to protect her clothing and a large hat with a veil that covered her whole face.

One of her favorite places to go in the car was to Seaside, Oregon. Mrs. Pittock and her nieces would ride in the chauffer-driven car and they'd stay for a month or more at a time. The chauffer would drive them all over the coast area sightseeing. Georgiana's nieces kept her young at heart: they even encouraged her to go and see a movie at the Seaside Theatre and when Henry came to town he went too. When they got back to Portland and the nieces told what they had done, other family members were shocked. They felt that Mr. and Mrs. Pittock should not do such things as it was considered "beneath them" to go to a movie house.

Georgiana loved to be on the go and even after she had a stroke, until close to the end of her life, she would still enjoy a good long ride around the perimeter of her beloved Portland.

Georgiana in her favorite hat, one she wore on many occasions—even on a trip to Mount Hood.

Chapter Seven:
Pittock Mansion

Sometime after the turn of the century, Mr. and Mrs. Pittock started thinking about building their new home in the west hills of Portland. Henry had first noticed this particular piece of land when he came down the Columbia River in a ship. He would often hike up into the west hills just to view the town that he loved. For the rest of his life he was fascinated with the view from this point. Not only could he watch the growth of the city but he could see two rivers and five mountain peaks as well.

Henry eventually bought the land, 46 acres in all, in the area known as Imperial Heights and was very proud of his purchase. The fact that Imperial Heights was also known as Lovers' Lane is not known to have influenced his judgment!

The story has been told that he would brag that he bought the land for $1.00 per acre. What he didn't say was that the man who owned the property had political aspirations and made Henry agree to *The Oregonian*'s editorial support if he ever decided to run for an office. Henry and Georgiana decided to build their new home. Why did they make a decision to build a mansion at this stage in their life? History has not shared that secret with us. Some people believe that Henry wanted more privacy; others felt that he wanted to build a home to be remembered by. Some maintain it was to keep up with the other millionaires in the Portland area who were building huge mansions, including his daughter, Caroline Pittock Leadbetter.

This photograph, taken soon after Pittock Mansion was constructed, shows the Mansion in the background, with the Gate Lodge in the foreground.

It took five years for the mansion to be built and when it was completed in 1914 it was a beautiful site to see, standing proud and tall on the point. This French Renaissance Revival Chateauesque style home had every new invention known to man at the time, including an elevator, indirect lighting, a walk-in refrigerator and a central vacuum system.

Chapter Seven: Pittock Mansion

Henry and Georgiana's home was built primarily with materials from the Northwest, out of pride for the region. He enjoyed proving that a person could have a truly Northwest home that was as beautiful as any on the east coast or Europe.

Pittock Mansion today, one hundred years since construction was completed. Now it's Portland's much-loved house museum, the jewel in a 46-acre setting of trees and wilderness trails close to the heart of the city.

It's interesting to note that Mrs. Pittock did not want to move to Imperial Heights as she felt it was too isolated and no one would come to see her. Her wishes were for a Colonial brick house closer to town.

The 16,000 square foot home was built to accommodate all of the extended Pittock family including the husbands of Kate and Lucy, as well as Lucy's three children and Georgiana's nieces.

The Queen of Portland's Roses

Eleven people in all lived there, making it feel more like a home than a mansion. Each family had their own wing that was interconnected with the rest of the house.

Chapter Seven: Pittock Mansion

Portraits of Henry L. Pittock and Georgiiana Burton Pittock
at about the age when they began to plan
their mansion on Imperial Heights .

It was a full and happy home filled with the laughter of children. Pittock grandson Robert "Peter" Gantenbein was born on moving day and it is fitting that he was the last of Georgiana's descendants to live in the mansion.

The house was furnished with pieces from their old house and some items were purchased from the Meier and Frank department store, since Meier and Frank made it clear that they would pull their advertising from *The Oregonian* if Henry didn't buy from them.

LIFE AT PITTOCK MANSION

The day began at breakfast, which always started with grapefruit in the breakfast room at 8 am as Henry considered it healthful. He was definitely in favor of anything that was considered healthful—once he even tried an electric bath to clear his sinuses. The original sketch of the mansion, now hanging on the wall in the lower level, shows an orangerie (a solarium) where citrus fruits could be grown indoors.

Himmi, the family's Chinese cook, came with the Pittocks when they moved to Imperial Heights. But the temptation to sneak up the nifty back stairway to the maids' room on the third floor was too powerful to resist and unfortunately Himmi was fired on the spot.

Georgiana had a chauffer named Herman Hawkinson, who took her wherever she wanted to go. So she did enjoy an almost daily ride into Portland and often took her two nieces with her.

Chapter Seven: Pittock Mansion

The Pittocks owned land where Mall 205 stands now and Mrs. Pittock loved to go to the nut orchard that they owned there. They'd often stop for treats at Strohecker's market on the way back. When she did not feel like going out, Herman would bring people to visit with her at the mansion.

A professional seamstress would come to the mansion and often stay for weeks at a time, to fit, measure and sew clothes for Georgiana.

Henry, the quintessential outdoorsman, blazed miles of trails on his property and named them all. The trail closest to the home, and no doubt closest to his heart, was called the Georgiana Trail. It was very much a wilderness property: bears were a common site at the mansion, often coming in from the woods looking for a drink of water.

In the evening everyone would gather in the library around the fire to visit, play games and read *The Oregonian* newspaper. On hot nights in summer, the grandchildren would pitch a tent on the sun porch to stay cool. If they listened carefully, they could hear the lions roaring in their cages at the zoo!

The mansion was a magnificent place to hold a wedding! When daughter Kate was married to Lockwood Hebard, she made a dramatic entrance down the white marble staircase from the second floor to meet her husband-to-be.

Granddaughter Rhoda Jane Gantenbein was also married there and it was the event of the season. An orchestra was hired to play in the downstairs billiard room, but when it was found that the room was not large enough, they reassembled in the basement corridor surrounding the billiard room and stood behind windows opening into the room.

Grandchildren were adored and given plenty of free rein. The Pittocks were indulgent grandparents. The mansion was a fascinating place, a children's paradise, inside and out.

Christmas at Pittock Mansion was a splendid event. Homemade gifts were assembled, including candy and treats. Taffy was pulled, twisted, then wrapped in squares of crinkly waxed paper until, piece by piece, enough was made to fill a small gift box.

It was a tradition that the holiday turkey would be filled with two different kinds of stuffing, one at each end. And speaking of traditions, Bourbon Balls were always a favorite and no one could ever keep track of how many splashes of bourbon were added!

So many family members and friends came to dinner that the long dining table was carried into the music room and smaller tables were set up for the youngsters.

When guests with children came to visit, the children were allowed to search the dining room paneling to find the secret compartment where the silver was stored. It was a marvelous way to keep the children occupied and from family reports we learn that the secret wasn't discovered until they were adults.

Chapter Seven: Pittock Mansion

(from left) Portland architect, Al Staehli, the author, Janet Wilson, and William Burton Barry (son of Louise Burton Barry who lived with her Aunt Georgie at the mansion) completed a successful search for a secret compartment in the mansion's paneling.

Now that Georgiana and Henry were living in elegant surroundings, it was time that they had their portraits painted, to hang in this magnificent house. Mrs. Pittock sat still for many hours as the artist worked on her likeness.

However Henry had so much nervous energy that he could not sit still. He kept tap-tapping a pencil so much that it annoyed the artist—who retaliated by painting a portrait of Henry holding a pencil.

The artist worked diligently, using mathematical computations to be certain that the Pittock's eyes would be focused on viewers, no matter where they stand.

83

The Queen of Portland's Roses

The portraits, which now hang in the upstairs hall at Pittock Mansion, originally hung in the main floor library, on either side of the pocket doors leading to the hall and music room. Henry's brother, Robert, once asked why they were hanging there, of all places and Henry replied, "I want my Georgiana right here where I can see her!"

Chapter Eight:
Georgiana's Grandchildren

The Pittock grandchildren were much loved by everyone in their home and extended families. They must have had a grand time growing up in their beautiful home atop Imperial Heights—the spot Henry first saw when he first came down the Columbia River into Portland. This is the location where he and Georgiana dreamed of building a grand home with a view of the mountains and rivers, a home that they would share with pride, with his family and his decedents.

They longed for a home with enough room to house their multi-generational family, a home where they could live together instead of their smaller individual homes in the downtown area of the city. Their dream home would be a house that they hoped would stand forever, built to last for many generations.

This was a time of plenty for all of the family. Everyone was prospering, families were growing and times were good. Trips and outings for the whole family were numerous. Their philosophy was the more the merrier! The car was always full and the Pittocks all seemed to get along well on their family road trips. They'd pack a picnic lunch and be off to roam around Oregon, from the coast of Seaside to Mt. Hood and beyond.

The Queen of Portland's Roses

The family enjoyed taking the train to see the World's Fairs, wherever they might be held. There were trips to the Hotel Del Coronado in San Diego, Santa Barbara, Yellowstone Park, and their Uncle Tom's home on Neville Island, Pennsylvania. Mexico, England and even Hawaii, were a few of their holiday destinations. Life was an adventure and we know that the Pittock family members were definitely adventurous.

It has been said that the children were well behaved and wanted for nothing. Their nanny was reasonably lenient, and considered it her duty to amuse them when they were young. However, as, coddled as the children might have been, they did have rules, such as a requirement that they always finish breakfast and a restriction against using the elevator.

Breakfast was very important in the home and the meal started with good old vitamin C in its original form. Henry was a strong proponent of citrus, believing it to be a very healthy food. When it came to his children and grandchildren, he was in favor of anything that was deemed healthful. It has been said that little Georgiana was made to sit at the breakfast table until she finished her breakfast— and that occasionally took a very long time!

During the summer months they could all play games outside on the lawn, play hide and seek in the woods or the greenhouses, and play tennis on the dirt-floored tennis court. They even had their own play house near the point. Having sleepovers with friends out on the top floor terrace, under tents, was a favorite activity for these popular children.

Chapter Eight: Georgiana's Grandchildren

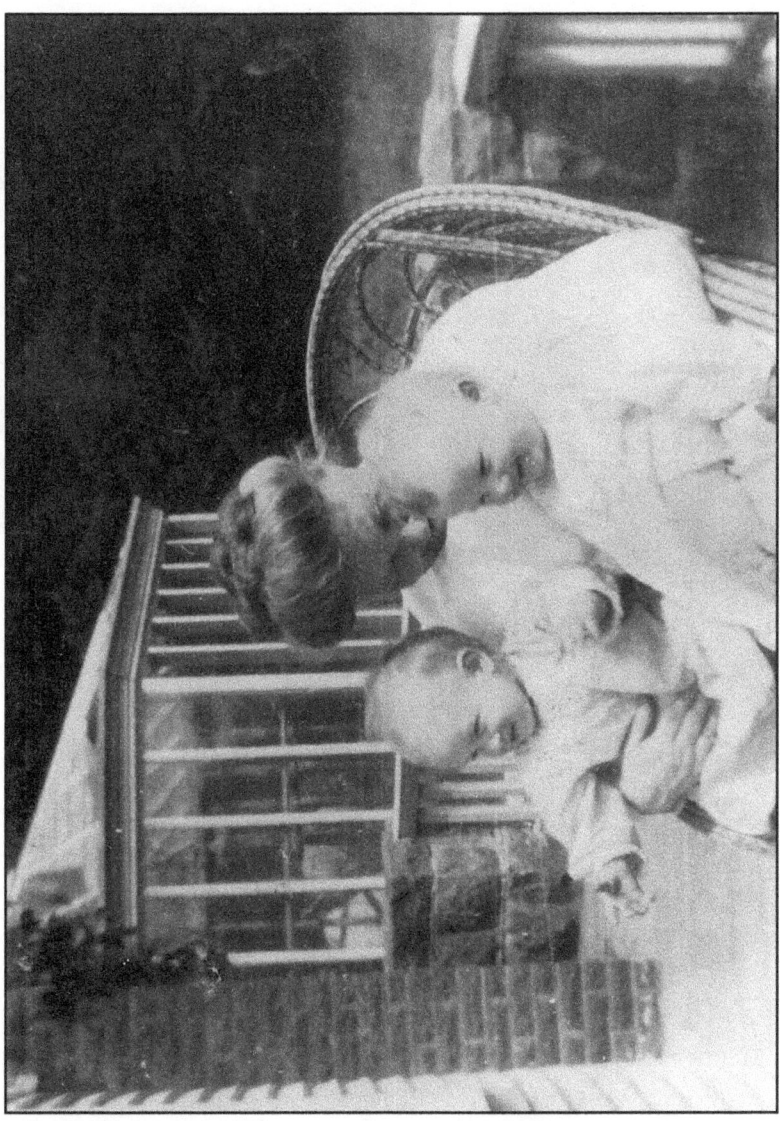

Georgiana, the doting grandmother, cuddling two plump baby granddaughters from her son Fred's family. This picture was taken at Lakeside, Lacamas Lake, Camas, Washington.

The Queen of Portland's Roses

The Pittocks were always on the go. On a visit to Santa Barbara, California, the young Pittocks visited their Leadbetter cousins.

Another fun summer activity was vacationing at Camas, Washington. The combined families had four separate homes around Camas Lake: Hornet's Nest, Fern Lodge, Lakeside and Pomeria. This is where most of the grandchildren learned to swim, sail, horseback ride, hunt, and water ski. It was like a private retreat for the whole family.

The children remember having caged pet raccoons that they would feed raw eggs to for breakfast. A favorite pastime for everyone was to fish on the lake and fry the catch for dinner. For the adults, it was fashionable to wear a suit and tie while fishing, but the children did not have to comply with this rigid dress code.

Chapter Eight: Georgiana's Grandchildren

During the long wet winters, the play was mostly indoors and the top floor of the mansion, which was a storage area, was turned into a play land with puppets, dolls, and even tricycles. Birthday parties were even held here.

Fern Lodge, at Lacamas Lake near Camas, Washington, where the Pittock grandchildren enjoyed summer activities.

One birthday party included a band for dancing, with everyone being allowed to use the elevator to go up and down--which was such a big hit! This was also a popular spot to go to after school. The children were allowed to call down to the kitchen on the house intercom and ask the cook to send up sandwiches, cookies and milk for them in the dumb waiter.

Hide and seek was a popular game inside the house, too, with so many places to hide on each and every floor. When the grandchildren became bored with hiding and their parents still were visiting, their mothers told them to go play pirate.

The Queen of Portland's Roses

Bertha Pittock, Fred Pittock's wife, with their children:
(front, l to r) Virginia, Henry II, Fredrika,
(middle row, l to r) Barbara, Marjorie, Roberta.

They were instructed to find the two niches, full of the family's silver, that were hidden in the dining room. It wasn't until many years later that William Burton Berry (a Pittock great-nephew, son of one of the two nieces who lived with the

Chapter Eight: Georgiana's Grandchildren

Pittocks), Al Staehli, (long-time Pittock Mansion volunteer) and I actually located the niches in the buffet.

One of the chores that was everyone's duty, including the grandchildren's, was to check on the canary as they walked by its cage. The cage was situated on the second-floor landing near the bedrooms. Henry insisted that the little bird be there to alert his family to the presence of poisonous gasses in his home.

The electric light was a new invention and people were not sure if it created a toxic gas. Henry reasoned that if a canary could be used in the mines to identify the presence of gas, it would work in his home as well. Henry had a most inventive mind that produced fascinating solutions to many everyday problems.

Holiday time was special for the grandchildren. They enjoyed being allowed to help make the handmade and hand-wrapped candies. This was a tradition that all enjoyed. Pulling taffy seemed to be the job no one wanted as the taffy was so hot to handle.

There was always a huge tree to be found in the front hall landing, with presents underneath for all. Family members would come from near and far to celebrate, and they would be served a huge feast, including the traditional turkey with all the trimmings.

William Burton Barry (known as Billy Barry) and his brother Alexander were treated just like grandchildren too.

William remembers that he always was given the leg of the turkey on Thanksgiving, when he and the younger children ate at a different table in the Turkish smoking room. (He confided recently that he always hated the leg.)

Henry Lewis Pittock II and his sister, Marjorie

Reading was encouraged for all the grandchildren and they saw their family gather to read in the library almost every night after dinner. During my interview with grandson Peter Gantenbein's lifelong friend, Thomas Holman, Tom shared some interesting stories.

Chapter Eight: Georgiana's Grandchildren

Peter loved to read so much he often brought his own reading lamp to his friends' homes, so as to have good light to read by while he was visiting. On one occasion, he even took a comfortable chair and a favorite lamp all the way to the beach, so he would be well equipped for reading.

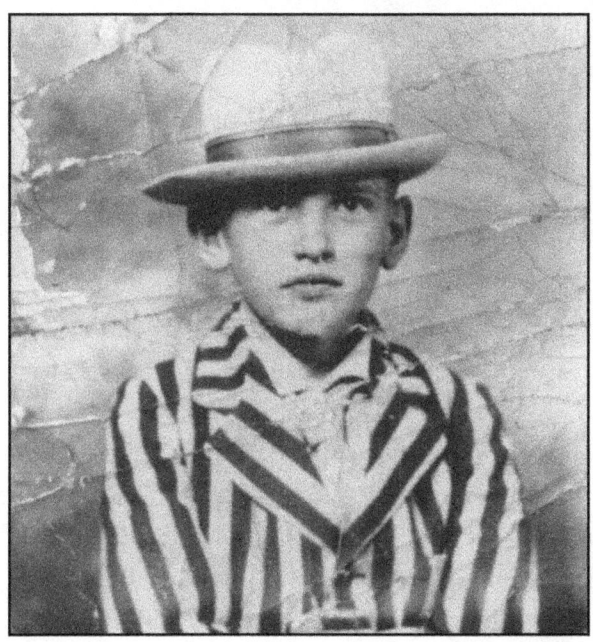

Peter Gantenbein, youngest child of Georgiana's and Henry's daughter Helen Louise "Lucy." Peter was born on the day his grandparents moved to their new mansion, and he was the last Pittock to live in the house.

Everyone enjoyed working on jigsaw puzzles and there were always several puzzles underway in the house at the same time, in different rooms. Crossword puzzles were also popular with the family and a dictionary was always on hand to settle arguments.

The Queen of Portland's Roses

The Leadbetter clan, including some of Caroline Pittock Leadbetter's children.

The circus was great entertainment for the grandchildren, and Henry, always made sure that they received tickets to all the events in town including the ever-favorite circus. This was the event everyone waited to see. The animals from all over the world fascinated the children.

Roller-skating was allowed on the marble floors in the entry. The grandchildren enjoyed sliding down the banister, and going up and down the dumbwaiter after being told that the elevator was for their Grandmothers' use only and not for play. Descendants remember even today a birthday party that includ a fishing game, where the children leaned over the second floor handrail and used real fishing poles to "catch" and reel in presents off the bottom floor of the mansion.

Chapter Eight: Georgiana's Grandchildren

Oh, what an enchanting time it must have been for the youngsters, to sit at their grandmother's knee and hear stories of how she met her husband while driving her surrey up and down the two streets of Portland. Or to hear her tell of her adventures crossing the plains, stories replete with Indians, famine, cholera, and floods. Yet Georgiana Pittock lived to see automobiles, telephones and airplanes flying over Portland. So much had changed for them in just one lifetime! The family was growing and the times were changing, very quickly.

I am so thankful that we have many pictures, genealogy charts, and oral interviews from the extended Pittock and Leadbetter families from which to pull such valuable formation that enables us to piece the past together the past and let us get to know the family better.

Fred & Bertha Pittock's children (l. to r.):
Virginia, Marjorie, Barbara, Roberta, Fredrika and Henry II.

95

The Queen of Portland's Roses

Several of Georgiana's and Henry's grandchildren lined up for a photograph at Imperial Heights: *(from left)*
Henry Pittock II, Peter and Georgiana Gantenbein,
Fredrika and Roberta Pittock, friend Catherine Deyette Eva, Barbara,
Marjorie and Virginia Pittock.

Chapter Nine:
Georgiana's Legacy

Unfortunately, the elder Pittocks did not have long to enjoy their mansion. Georgiana had been ill following a stroke that occurred just prior to the completion of the mansion, one that had left her partially paralyzed. An elevator was not on the original plans but was installed in the mansion as an afterthought, so that Mrs. Pittock could move around her home. Since moving into her new home, she had been slowly fading.

On June 12, 1918 Georgiana Martin Burton Pittock passed away peacefully in her home on Imperial Heights, from complications of her stroke. She must have known that her time was coming to leave this earth because she had asked her daughter Lucy to have her nieces come to see her. Lucy told Helen and Louise to let Aunt Georgie talk to them about the old days as this was something that Georgiana liked to do. It was at this time that Georgiana gave her favorite broach to Louise and her favorite ring to Helen. The broach is still in the Burton family and I have held it in my hand.

Upon her death, Georgiana was laid out in her bedroom so that family and friends could come to the mansion to pay their respects to a woman who was loved by all. Family members

The Queen of Portland's Roses

have told me stories of how the grandchildren lined up at the bottom of the stairs waiting their turn to go and kiss their Grandmother good-bye.

Both Georgiana and Henry Pittock (who died shortly after his wife, on January 28, 1919, during an outbreak of influenza) are buried at River View Cemetery, in Portland. Their graves are surrounded by others that bear names from the pages of Oregon history.

Georgiana Pittock, in the final years of her life, posed for this photograph in the Music Room at Pittock Mansion.

When Mrs. Pittock died, her estate was overseen by her husband Henry L Pittock until his untimely death a few months later.

Chapter Nine: Georgiana's Legacy

Georgiana Pittock's last public appearance before her death on June 12, 1918. Mrs. Pittock had suffered from a stroke several years earlier.

The Queen of Portland's Roses

When Henry passed, the entire estate had not been settled so it was left to their oldest son Frederick Pittock to petition the court to distribute the remaining monies to the family. This did not occur until 1924. At that time Mrs. Pittock had $30,318.67 in cash in her bank account with no real property.

After paying $751.00 for her own funeral, an appraisal fee of $3.00 and court expenses of $8.50 the balance was distributed, by law, with $14,778.00 going to her late husband's estate and the balance divided equally among five of her children:

> Susan P. Emery, Hillsboro, Pennsylvania
>
> Fred F. Pittock, 570 Hawthorne Terrace Portland, Oregon
>
> Carrie P. Leadbetter, 795 Park Avenue Portland, Oregon
>
> Kate P. Hebard, Imperial Heights Portland, Oregon
>
> Helen Louise P. Gantenbein, Imperial Heights, Portland, Oregon

The process was overseen by Henry's male secretary, Mr. Ora Lee Price, and only Henry's share of the estate was taxed in the amount of $97.78. The children's share was exempt in taxes up to $5,000. Fred Pittock did not charge for his services to administer the monies.

Henry and Georgiana Pittock are buried at River View Cemetery, Portland, Oregon.

Chapter Nine: Georgiana's Legacy

Mrs. Pittock was unusual in that she had her own money and her own bank account. Most women of the day let their husbands handle all the finances but then our Georgiana was no ordinary woman.

The Pittock family lived in the mansion until 1958, when Robert "Peter" Gantenbein was the last relative to leave. Peter had never married. The home was too large for him and the property taxes had gone up considerably. The remaining grandchildren divided up the furniture, saving the pieces they wanted. Then, in 1960, a huge sale was held at the mansion and the rest of the furnishings were sold. Peter put the mansion up for sale.

The home was in need of many repairs when Peter left but even more repairs were needed after the Columbus Day storm in 1962 that nearly destroyed the Pittock home. The mansion was sitting empty when the storm hit. Trees were knocked down, roof tiles blown away and windows broken. Many people in the area felt the home could never be repaired, but others remained optimistic. It wasn't until after the city of Portland acquired the home that the repairs were started. The first task was to seal up the home and start the furnace, to attempt to dry it out after its exposure to the wet and windy weather.

The city acquired the home from the family for $225,000 in 1964, with the help of the people of Portland who did not want the mansion to be destroyed. Many of the craftsmen who had built the mansion were still around to help with the repairs, since Henry had hired many young craftsmen (some just out of school) to build his home, and so they were still alive in the 60's to help restore the fabulous building.

But it took over a year to undo the damage caused when the home had been left open for years to the elements. The floors had warped, and moss and mildew grew on the marble and plaster.

Thus the home was saved from a building contractor who was anxious to tear it down and build smaller homes in its place. By 1965 the mansion had been repaired sufficiently to allow the public in to see the estate, Furniture was donated by some of the wealthiest people in Portland, and furniture of the era of Georgiana and Henry (prior to 1919) was displayed. Volunteers were recruited to give tours of the home. Pittock Mansion was on its way to becoming one of Portland's most popular tourist spots.

Over the years the mansion has been open to the public, thousands of visitors have been welcomed into Georgiana's and Henry's home by hundreds of volunteers and staff. After taking a tour, guests carry away a better vision of what life was like in an era that is long gone and a life style known to only a few.

GEORGIANA"S LEGACY

Women of Mrs. Pittock's time usually were over shadowed by their husbands especially when they were as industrious as, Henry Lewis Pittock. (Side bar) At the time of Henry's death he had an interest in at least 65 different companies.

Chapter Nine: Georgiana's Legacy

However, Georgiana was not over shadowed because not only did Georgiana marry a remarkable man … Henry married a remarkable woman.

Georgiana was popular among the ladies and everyone trusted her and her judgment saying that, she was one of the greatest ladies to ever live. It has been written that once you were her friend you were always her friend. She kept friends for a lifetime.

Portland is a better place to live because of Mrs. Pittock and her desire to make a difference in the lives of the people. A person could never know all the lives she must have touched both child and adult, with her charity work. Some may have been touched in a small way and others in a life changing way. Some may have been touched enough to carry on the tradition.

Many of her favorite charities are still in existence and growing. These loving intuitions might be needed even more now then they were back then.

The Portland Rose Festival has grown tremendously. The Grand Floral Parade is huge and is televised nationally. We even have an air show now. What would Georgiana think? Who would have thought that little trip to England to see the roses would go so far. She would be proud.

I am so pleased that Georgiana lived long enough to see women win the right to vote. It was a long time coming and she worked tirelessly on the endeavor. I can visualize the ladies singing in the streets when the votes were counted.

Mrs. Georgiana Martin Burton Pittock was an incredible woman in her time and certainly would be in our time, as well.

A Pittock Family Album

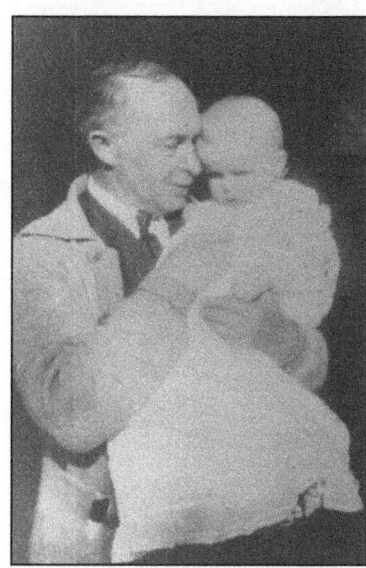

Fred Francis with son, young Henry II

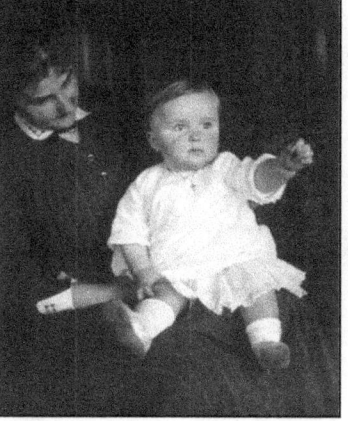

(above) Henry Pittock at Multnomah Falls

(at right) Young Henry Pittock II

The Queen of Portland's Roses

Baby Henry II, like all the grandchildren, was adored by their Pittock grandparents.

Bertha holding young Henry Pittock II.

Henry Pittock II plays in his "fort" in front of the family's Hawthorne Terrace home.

Pittock Family Album

The beautiful Gantenbein sisters, Rhoda *(at top)* and Georgiana were Pittock granddaughters. They were the daughters of Helen Louise ("Lucy") Pittock.

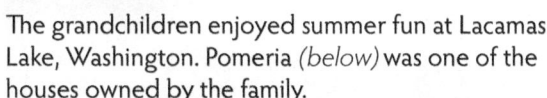

The grandchildren enjoyed summer fun at Lacamas Lake, Washington. Pomeria *(below)* was one of the houses owned by the family.

The Queen of Portland's Roses

(above) Twins Charles & Louise Gallien with their Aunt Van Houten

(at right) Mr. & Mrs. C L Gallien, parents of the twins

(below) Lucy & Ed Gantenbein

Pittock Family Album

Fred and Bertha ("Bird") Pittock surrounded by children.

Virginia Pittock with baby sis, Fredrika

Pittock children at Lakeside with Aunt Fannie Leadbetter

The Queen of Portland's Roses

Susan Pittock Emery, Georgiana and Henry's daughter, in her later years, receiving a certificate of appreciation for her charitable work.

For Georgiana, consideration for the plight of those less fortunate was a guiding principle throughout her life. She encouraged her son and daughters to follow in her footsteps. In the photograph below, tiny Caroline Pittock Leadbedder is thanked for her contribution.

At the Portland docks, 1936, seeing off Peter Gantenbein and his friend, Tom Holman, traveling to Japan, were *(l. to r.)* Ethyl Holman, Georgiana Gantenbein Aston, Elizabeth Holman McIndoe (Tom's twin) and Lucy Pittock Gantenbein.

This picture was taken in the basement of the Old Oregonian Bldg, on the inauguration of the first color press .1940-1941. *(front row, l. to r.)*: Jimmie Brooks with open paper, Mike Frey with open paper, and in center, Virginia P. Thorsen w/ Warren Jr. Bird has a feather in her hat, behind Susan Emery. Next, O.L. Price and Fred Emery with pipe. Henry L Pittock II is behind Fred Emery, far right. Newspaper staff is in back row.

The Queen of Portland's Roses

(at left) Fred Pittock with his two youngest children, Fredrika and Henry Lewis Pittock II

(at right) Henry Pittock, pencil in hand, looks down on son, Fred, and grandbaby, Warren Thorsen Jr. *(below)* Virginia Thorsen with Warren Jr. and baby Teddy.

Pittock Family Album

At Roberta Pittock's Wedding to Boyd Macnaughton *(l. to r.)*: Boyd, Henry Lewis Pittock III, Trudy MacNaughtton (the groom's mother), Sally Leadbetter (Fred's sister), Roberta, John McDougal (Marjorie's husband) & Virginia Pittock Thorsen.

Smiling baby Teddy Thorsen.

Peggy Pittock with children *(l. to r.)* Diane, Peter and Henry L. Pittock III.

The Queen of Portland's Roses

Henry Pittock II's childhood home,
Camas, Washington

(below) Fred Leadbetter, Caroline's husband, with his mother, Annie, and his brother, Lewis

(below) Peter Gantenbein, in center, stands with friends un front of his sister, Rhoda Jane Gantenbein's green LaSalle, 1932, Gearhart, Oregon

Pittock Family Album

(right, l. to r.) Pittock great-granddaughter, Kate Mills, with her parents, Clemmie and Petie (Caroline's son, Henry Lewis Pittock Leadbetter)

(left) Henry Pittock II, donned a goatee and dressed up like his grandfather—a striking resemblance to the portrait of Henry. him.

(below, l. to r.) Pittock great-granddaughter, Nancy Dudley and Pittock grandaughter, centenarian Betty Meier, at the wake for Mrs. Meier's cousin, Henry Pittock II, 2007.

(at right) Virginia Pittock Thorsen, with her sons, Warren Jr. and Teddy, sits in front of the magnificent Povey window in the house at Hawthorne Terrace.

(below) Henry Pittock II took family and friends on a tour of the former Hawthorne Terrace family home, *(l. to r.)*: Glenna Pittock; the then-current owner's daughter; Suzanne Pittock; Henry Pittock III; Henry Pittock IV *(in back)*; Henry Pittock II *(in front)*,;Mrs. Angel (the owner); Peter Pittock; and the author, Janet Wilson.

Family Trees

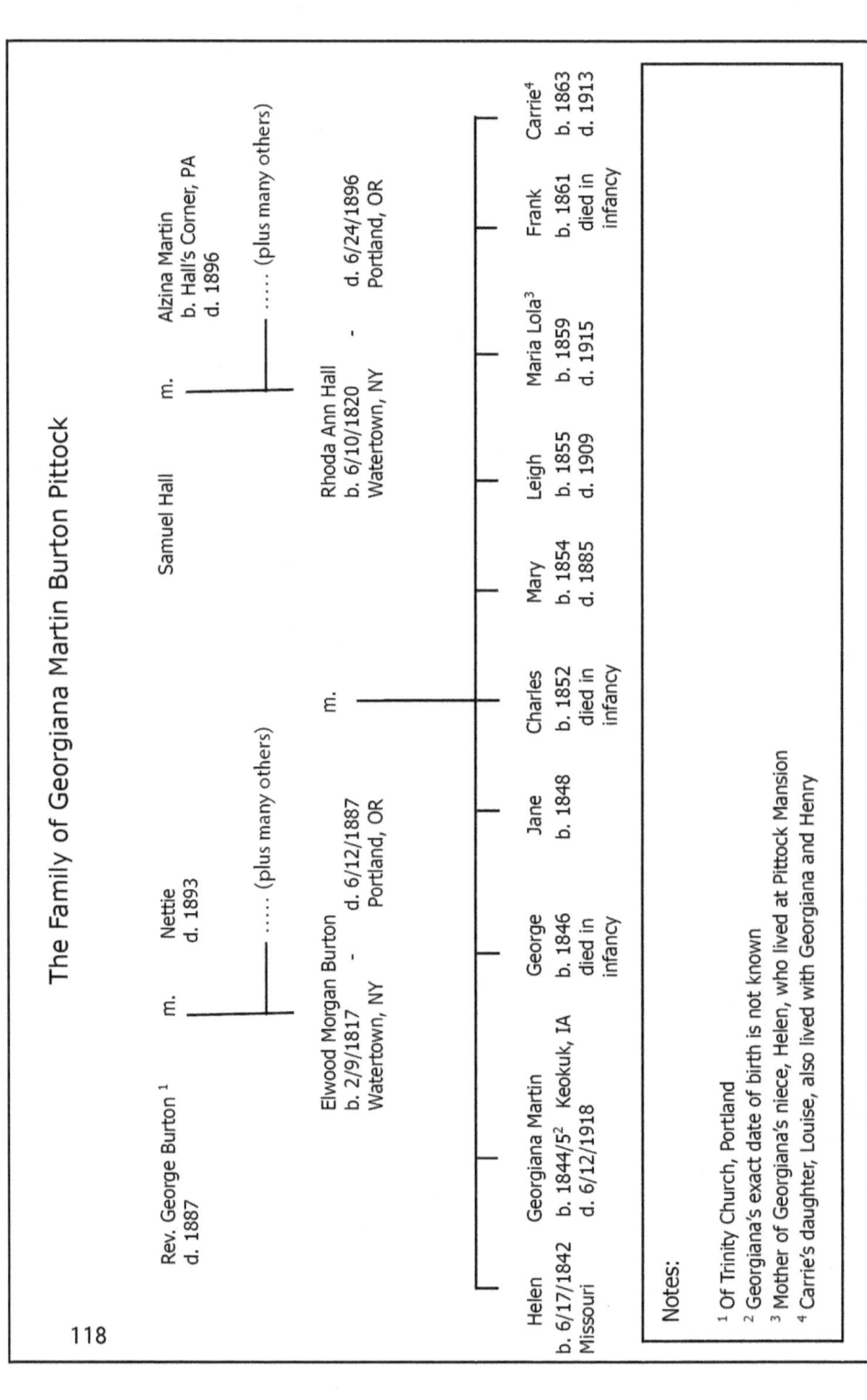

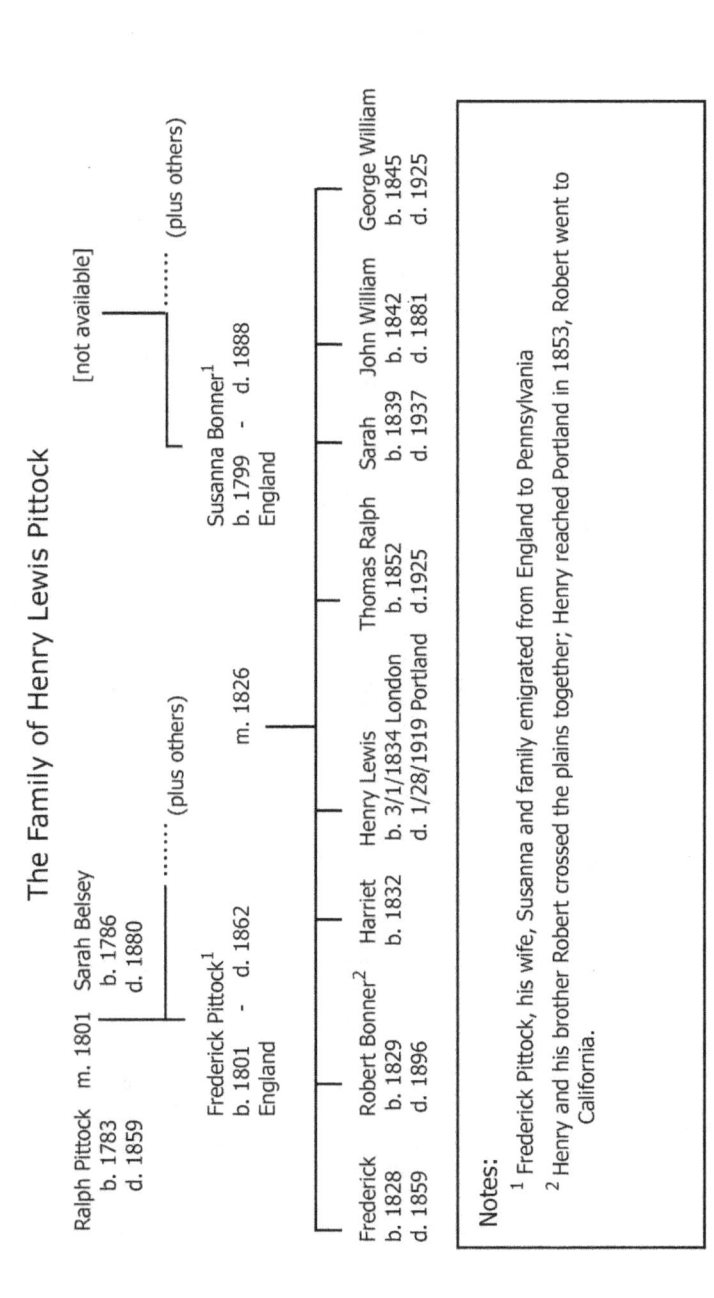

The Family of Henry Lewis Pittock

Ralph Pittock m. 1801 Sarah Belsey
b. 1783　　　　　　b. 1786
d. 1859　　　　　　d. 1880
　　　　　　　┅┅┅ (plus others)

Susanna Bonner[1]
b. 1799 - d. 1888
England
　　　　　　　┅┅┅ [not available]
　　　　　　　　　　┅┅┅ (plus others)

Frederick Pittock[1]　　m. 1826
b. 1801 - d. 1862
England

Frederick	Robert Bonner[2]	Harriet	Henry Lewis	Thomas Ralph	Sarah	John William	George William
b. 1828	b. 1829	b. 1832	b. 3/1/1834 London	b. 1852	b. 1839	b. 1842	b. 1845
d. 1859	d. 1896		d. 1/28/1919 Portland	d. 1925	d. 1937	d. 1881	d. 1925

Notes:

[1] Frederick Pittock, his wife, Susanna and family emigrated from England to Pennsylvania

[2] Henry and his brother Robert crossed the plains together; Henry reached Portland in 1853, Robert went to California.

The Family of Henry and Georgiana Pittock

Henry Lewis Pittock
b. 3/01/1834 England
d. 1/28/1919

m.

Georgiana Martin Burton
b. 1845-6* Keokuk, IA
d. 6/12/1918

Susan	Greta	Frederick Francis	Robert Elwood	Caroline Thuseba	Henry Lewis Jr.	Katherine Thorne "Kate"	Helen Louise "Lucy"	Harriet Lovell
b. 7/13/1861	b. 1862-3*	b. 1864	b. 1866	b. 1870	b. 1871	b. 1855	b. 1858	b. 1878
d. 3/16/1952		d. 1938	d. 1886	d. 1972	d. 1871	d. 1885	d. 1909	d. 1878

Notes:

* exact date of birth is not known.

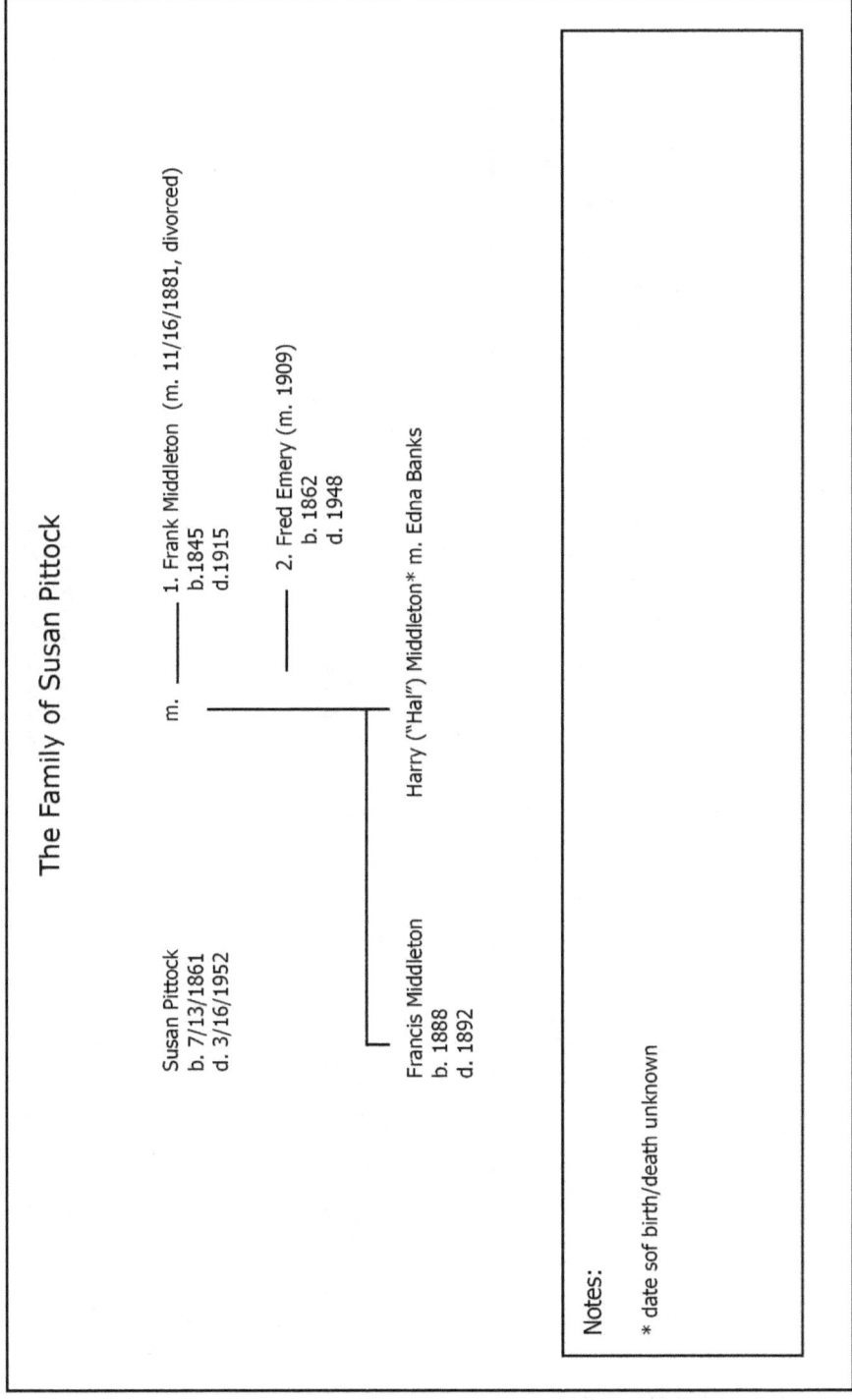

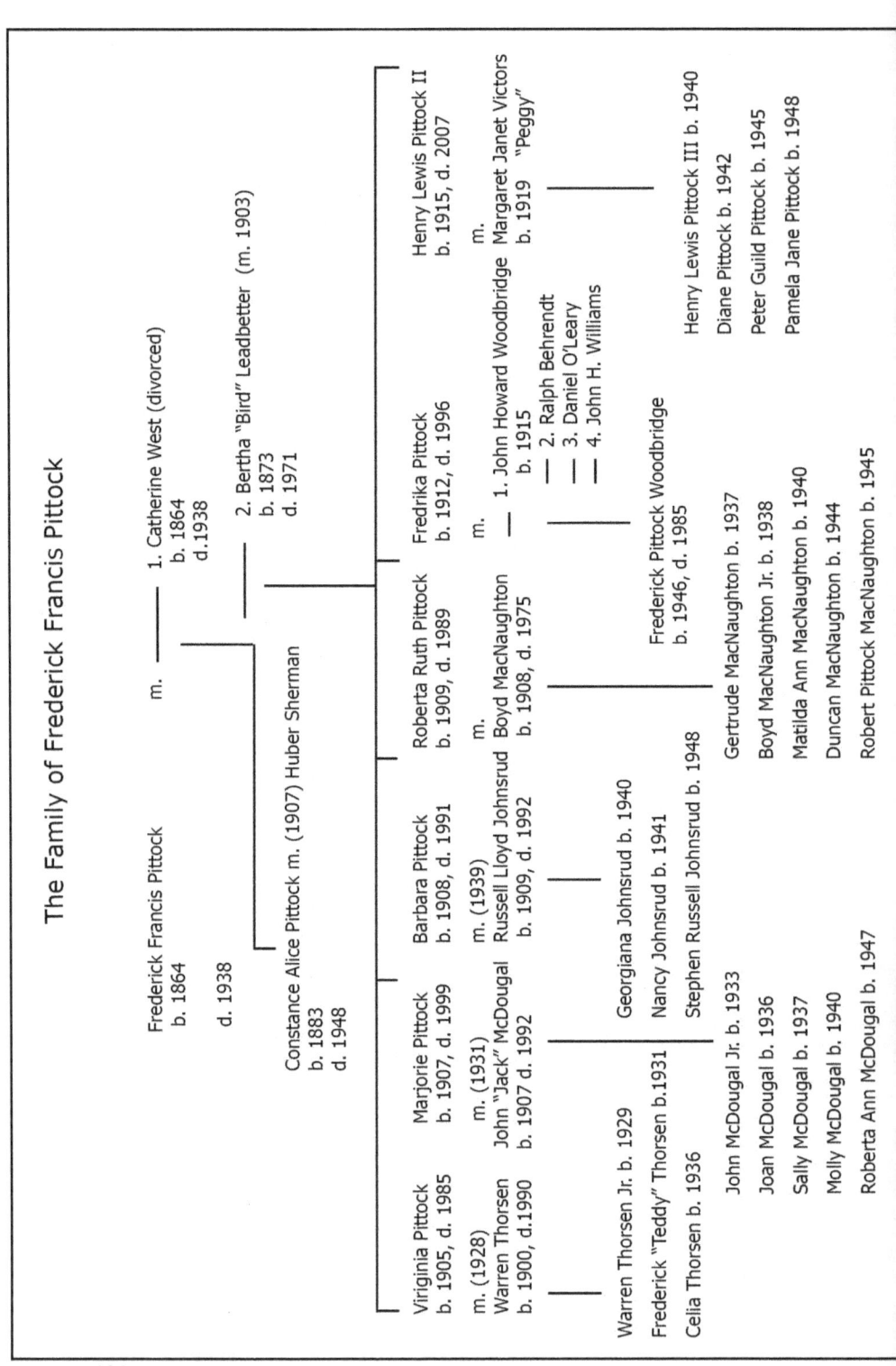

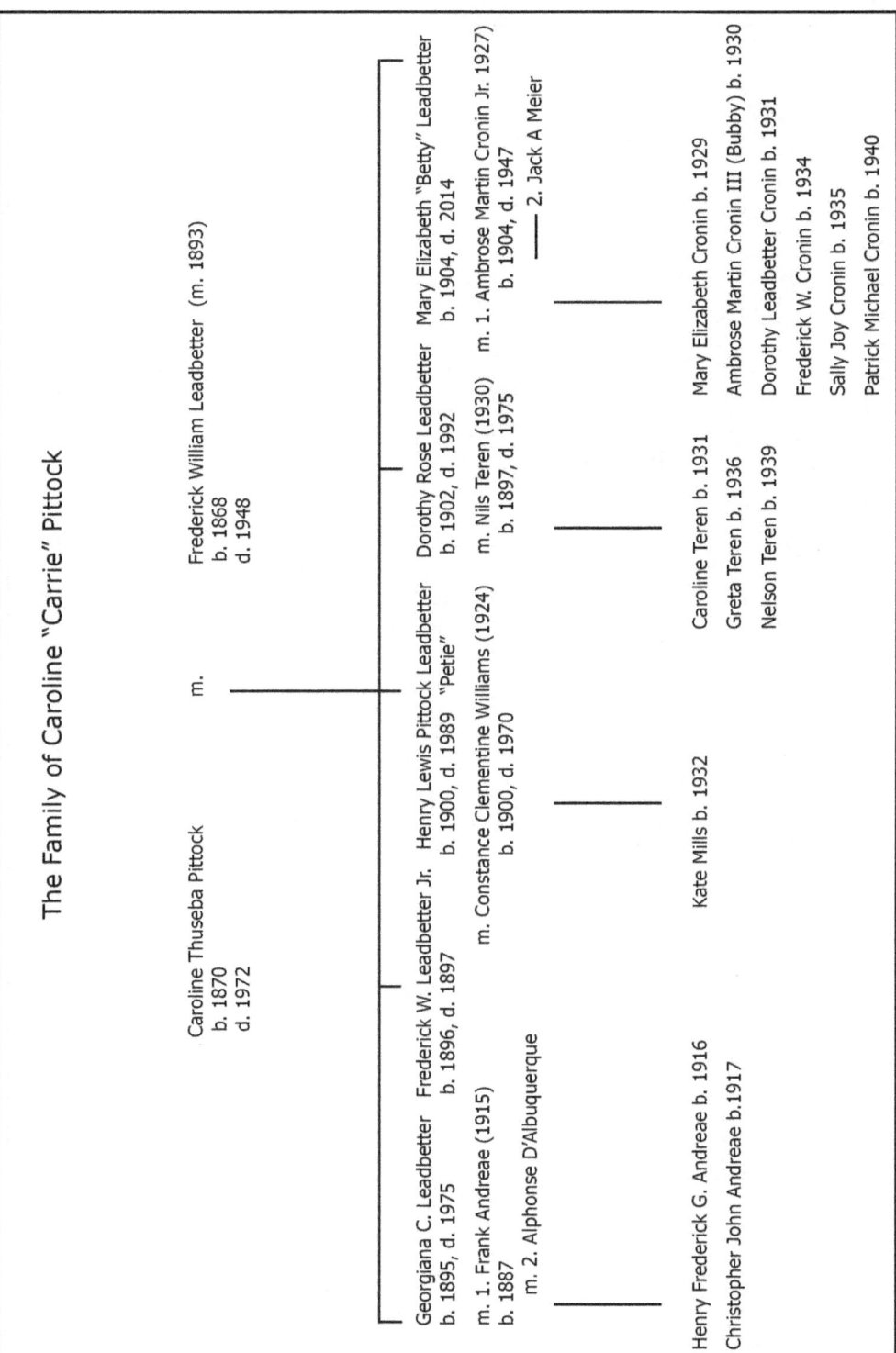

The Family of Katherine Thorne "Kate" Pittock

Katherine Thorne "Kate" Pittock   m.   ———   1. John Hertzman (m. 1900)
b. 1873   b. 1868
d. 1941   d. 1907

                                    ———   2. Lockwood Hebard* (m. 1914)

John Hamilton Hertzman
b. 1902, d. 1903

Notes:
*dates unknown

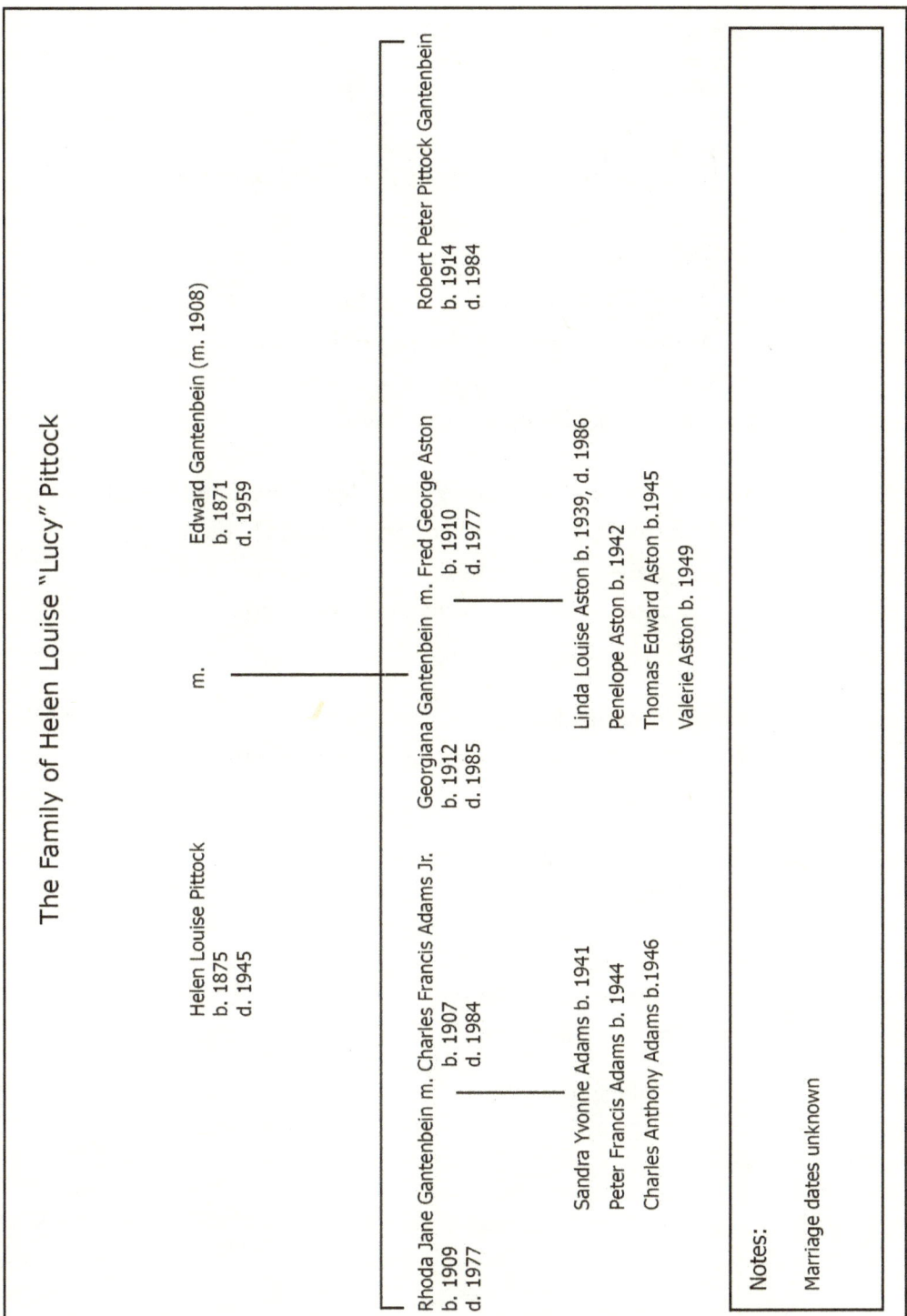

Visiting Pittock Mansion

Georgiana's home on Imperial Heights, now known as Pittock Mansion, is owned by the City of Portland. This elegant and well-loved house museum is operated by the Pittock Mansion Society and is open to the public.

See the rooms where Georgiana, Henry and family lived, diligently restored and furnished. Stroll through the gardens or hike the trails the Pittocks carved through the 46 acres of wooded paradise overlooking downtown Portland.

Pittock Mansion is located at:
3229 NW Pittock Drive, Portland, Oregon 97210

For information about hours and events:
Call (503) 823-3624

Or visit the Pittock Mansion website at:
www.pittockmansion.com

Sources

Joseph Gaston "Portland City of Roses," 1912

"Pittock Mansion Remembered", An Oral Interview with Louise Barry, 1984.

"Pittock Mansion Remembered:, An Oral Interview with Marjorie Skene Wright. " 1984.

Oral Interview with, Marjorie Pittock MacDougall, 1996. Pittock Mansion Archives.

Oral Interview with, Elizabeth Leadbetter Cronin Meier, 1996. Pittock Mansion Archives.

Oral Interview with, William Burton Barry, 1997. Pittock Mansion Archives.

Oral Interview with, Thomas Holman, 1997. Pittock Mansion Archives

Oral Interview with, Henry Lewis Pittock II, 2000. Pittock Mansion Archives.

Obituary of Georgiana Martin Burton Pittock, 1918

Last Will and Testament of Georgiana M. Pittock, 1918

Last Will and Testament of Henry Lewis Pittock, 1919

"Pharisee Among Philistines" by Malcolm Clark, Jr. 1975

Oregon Historical Society Library and Manuscripts Department

Index

A-C

Adams, Charles A, 125
Adams, Charles F. Adams 125
Adams, Rhoda Jane Gantenbein 35, 81, 107, 114, 125
Adams Peter F. 125
Adams, Sandra 125
Alzina Martin Hall 11
Andreae, Christopher 123
Andreae, Georgiana Leadbetter 32, 63, 123
Andreae, Frank 123
Andreae, Henry 123
Aston, Fred G. 125
Aston, Georgiana Gantenbein 35, 63, 86, 107, 111, 125
Aston, Linda Louise 125
Aston, Penelope 125
Aston, Thomas 125
Aston, Valerie 125
Baby Home 43, 44, 49
Barry, Alexander 37
Barry, William Burton 37, 83, 90, 91
Behrendt, Ralph 122
Boys' & Girls' Aid Society 46, 49
Burton, Charles 13
Burton, Elwood 11, 12, 14, 17, 24, 118
Burton, George 11, 13
Burton, Mary 13
Burton, Rhoda Ann Hall 11, 25, 28, 118
Children's Home 48, 49
Cronin, Ambrose Jr. 123
Cronin, Dorothy 123
Cronin, Frederick 123
Cronin, Mary Elizabeth 123
Cronin, Patrick 123
Cronin, Sally Joy 123

D-F

D'Albuquerque, Alphonse 123
Dudley, Nancy Johnsrud 115, 122
Emery, Fred 28, 29, 111, 121
Emery, Susan Pittock 23, 28, 29, 38, 44, 100, 110, 111, 120
Female Seminary, 17
Fern Lodge 88, 89
Fruit & Flower Day Care 42

G

Gallien, Carrie Burton 24, 35, 36, 37, 108, 118
Gallien, Charles 24, 36, 108
Gallien, Charles L. 36
Gallien, Elwood 24, 36
Gallien, Louise 24, 36, 37, 97, 108
Gantenbein, Edward 34, 108, 125
Gantenbein, Helen Louise "Lucy " Pittock 23, 34, 35, 44, 77, 100, 107, 108, 120, 125
Gantenbein, R. Peter 35, 80, 92, 93, 96, 101, 114, 125
Georgiana Gantenbein 96
Georgiana Steamer 63, 64
Georgiana Trail 81
Georgie Burton Steamer 59, 60, 61, 62

H-J

Hall, Alzina Martin 16, 25, 118
Hawkinson, Herman 80, 81
Hebard, Kate Pittock 24, 33, 34, 35, 77, 81, 100, 120, 124
Hebard, Lockwood 33, 34, 35, 81, 124
Hertzman, John 33, 124
Hertzman, John Hamilton 33, 124
Himmi 39, 80
Holman, Tom 92
Hornet's Nest 88
Imperial Heights 26, 71, 75, 85
Johnsrud, Barbara Pittock 30, 90, 95, 96, 122
Johnsrud, Georgiana 122
Johnsrud, Russell Lloyd, 122
Johnsrud, Stephen Russell 122

L-M

Lacamas Lake 67, 87, 89, 107
Ladies' Relief Society 40, 48
Ladies Sewing Society 40, 41, 43
Lakeside 87, 88, 109
Leadbetter, Annie 114
Leadbetter, Caroline Pittock 32, 33, 38, 67, 76, 94, 100, 110, 120, 123
Leadbetter, C. Clementine Williams 33
Leadbetter, Constance "Clemmie" Williams 115, 123
Leadbetter, Fannie 109
Leadbetter, Frederick Jr. 33, 123

Leadbetter, Frederick W. 32, 67, 114, 123
Leadbetter, Henry "Petie" 33, 123
Lewis & Clark Exposition 55, 67
Lucy Pittock Gantenbein. 111
MacNaughton, Boyd 113, 122
MacNaughton, Boyd Jr. 122
MacNaughton, Duncan 122
MacNaughton, Gertrude 122
MacNaughton, Matilda 122
MacNaughton, Robert 122
MacNaughton, Roberta Pittock 30, 90, 95, 113, 122
Maple Grove 27
Martha Washington Hotel 45
Mazamas 34, 67
McDougal, Joan 122
McDougal, John "Jack" 113, 122
McDougal, John Jr. 122
McDougal, Marjorie Pittock 30, 90, 92, 95, 96, 122
McDougal, Molly 122
McDougal, Roberta Ann 122
McDougal, Sally 122
Meier, Betty Cronin 33, 115, 123
Middleton, Francis 28, 121
Middleton, Frank 28, 121
Middleton, Harry "Hal" 28, 121
Mills, Kate 115, 123
Mr. & Mrs. C L Gallien, 108

N-P

National Women's Rights Convention 48
Nieces' Room 35
Old People's Home 49
O'Leary, Daniel 122
Oregonian 18, 19, 20, 33, 40, 47, 75
Oregon Trail 13
Parry Center for Children 47, 48, 49
Pittock, Bertha Leadbetter 30, 38, 90, 109, 106, 111, 122
Pittock Block 26, 27
Pittock, Catherine 30, 122
Pittock, Diane 31, 113, 122
Pittock, Fred Francis 23, 30, 38, 100, 105, 109, 112, 120
Pittock, Fredrika 90
Pittock, Glenna 116
Pittock, Greta 23, 29, 38, 120
Pittock, Harriet Lovell 35, 120
Pittock, Henry II 6, 23, 30, 31, 90, 92, 94, 95, 96, 105, 106, 112, 115, 116, 122, 132
Pittock, Henry III 31, 113, 116, 122, 132

Pittock, Henry IV 116
Pittock, Henry Lewis I 18, 19, 20, 21, 23, 26, 30, 34, 53, 59, 61, 63, 67, 68, 69, 71, 75, 77, 83, 85, 94, 98, 100, 102, 106, 112, 119, 120
Pittock, Henry Lewis Jr. 33, 120
Pittock Mansion 26, 35, 56, 71, 76, 77, 80, 82, 102, 126
Pittock, Peggy Victors 30, 31, 113, 122
Pittock, Pamela 31, 122
Pittock, Peter 31, 113, 116, 122
Pittock. Robert Elwood 24, 31, 120
Pittock, Suzanne 116
Pomeria 88, 107
Portland Academy 17
Portland Rose Festival 52, 54, 103
Portland Rose Society 52, 55
Portland Women's Union 48

S-T

Sherman, Constance Alice Pittock 30, 122
SS Lake Bonneville 64, 65
Staehli, Alfred 64, 65, 83, 91
Stumptown 14
Teren, Caroline 123
Teren, Dorothy Leadbetter 29, 33, 123
Teren, Greta 123
Teren, Nelson, 123
Teren, Nils 123
Thorsen, Celia 122
Thorsen, Frederick "Teddy" 112, 113, 116, 122
Thorsen, Virginia Pittock 30, 90, 95, 96, 109, 111, 112, 113, 116, 122
Thorsen, Warren 122
Thorsen, Warren Jr. 111, 122

U-W

Unitarian Church 23, 24, 34, 39, 40, 41, 51

V

Van Houten, Garret 36
Van Houten, Helen 97
Van Houten, Helen 11, 24, 36, 37, 108
Van Houten, Marie Lola Burton 24, 35, 36, 37, 118
Warren Jr. 116
Warren Thorsen Jr. 112
Waverly Baby Home 44
Williams, John H. 122
Woodbridge, Fredrika Pittock 30, 95, 96, 109, 112
Woodbridge, Frederick 122
Woodbridge, John Howard 122

Acknowledgments

I want to acknowledge and thank many people for helping me to write this book. The first person to thank would have to be my mother for encouraging me to be creative and to keep writing.

My second acknowledgment would be to the entire extended Pittock family for allowing me access to their family photos and genealogy. Their kindness and generosity has been monumental.

Thank you also to Pittock Mansion curator Lucy Smith McLean and the Pittock Mansion Society for allowing me access to the archives and permission to use photos.

Another acknowledgment goes to Erica Calkins for her expertise on roses and life in another era, with sincere thanks also to Pittock Mansion's senior horticulturist, Robin Akers and the Portland International Rose Test Garden's, Harry Landers.

A big thank you to all the charitable organizations that opened their doors to me during the years I was on the streets researching the life of Mrs. Pittock. All of these organizations were extremely helpful in allowing me access to their archives. They just turned me loose to read and study for hours on end. These organizations include the Unitarian Church, Fruit and

Flower Day Care, The Old Church, Baby/Children's Home, The Boys and Girls Aid Society, and the Perry Center.

Last, but not least, a thank you to my editor Heather Kibbey for telling me, "You've got a book in you," and encouraging me to do something about it.

Janet L. Wilson

Author Janet L. Wilson is seen here (r. to l.) in with three Henry Pittocks: a bronze bust of Georgiana's husband Henry, their grandson the late Henry Pittock II and his son Henry III.

About the Author

Historian Janet L. Wilson has been researching the life of Georgiana Burton Pittock since the 1980s. A few years later she accepted a seat on the Board of Directors of the Pittock Mansion Society, serving until 2001. She has come to know her subject exceedingly well and has enjoyed a close friendship with the Pittock family.

Of Oregon pioneer stock herself (her ancestors crossed the Oregon Trail in 1848 and founded the city of Drain), Janet Wilson has long been interested in preserving Oregon's heritage and has conscientiously been recording oral interviews of those who can carry the thread of history to future generations.

The Queen of Portland's Roses
The Life of Georgiana Burton Pittock

is available at book and gift stores.

You may also enjoy

A Plant List of the Pittock Mansion Gardens

Sharing the trade secrets of Pittock Mansion's magnificent borders!
Here are the common and botanical names of the plants you see at Pittock, border by border.

Available at the Pittock Mansion Museum Shop and at book and gift stores.

Panoply Press
PO Box 1885
Lake Oswego, Oregon, 97035
panoplypress@gmail.com

www.ingramcontent.com/pod-product-compliance
Lightning Source LLC
LaVergne TN
LVHW011424080426
835512LV00005B/242